LENT AND EASTER WITH THE CHURCH FATHERS

Marco Pappalardo

Libreria Editrice Vaticana

United States Conference of Catholic Bishops
Washington, D.C.

First printing, January 2010

ISBN 978-1-60137-087-7

CONTENTS

For those who live

each day with hope

and a contemplative

gaze, confident that

"all things work for good

for those who love God"

(Rom 8:28).

INTRODUCTION

The Holy Father Pope Benedict XVI, in his Wednesday general audiences from March 2007 through a good part of the year 2008, undertook the journey of presenting the Church Fathers. It was a steady and profound catechesis in the full sense of the word, recounting the story of the Church through the lives of men who were important personalities during the first centuries of Christianity. Each time, attention was given to highlighting the originality, and at the same time the modern relevance, of each Church Father—some of whom are unknown to most people—so that he could instead become accessible to everyone.

This book has been conceived with the same idea: aiming to present with great simplicity the thoughts and meditations of some of the Church Fathers regarding the key seasons of the liturgical year. The Fathers' writings are in fact among the most important traditional documents, in terms of the richness of their content on multiple levels: spiritual, moral, dogmatic, and ascetic. Following the path laid by the Holy Father's intuition, the idea of this book is to "draw out" the Church Fathers from the libraries or patristic archives in order to offer them to everyone, including those who are neither specialists, nor scholars, nor aficionados. In fact, this small book is not a text for study. It is intended to be a tool, even a daily companion, for meditation during Lent and the Easter season.

Anyone wishing to study these extraordinary men in greater depth can find works of great value, dense and impressive collections of their writings, monumental volumes, and monographic texts that are increasingly easy to access.

Each passage in this book is supplied with an introduction in italics by the author, in order to provide a key to interpreting the selection and to bring the content to life for the modern reader.

Marco Pappalardo

MEDITATIONS

From Ash Wednesday to the Saturday after Ash Wednesday

Ash Wednesday

Augustine, *Tractates on the Gospel of St. John*, 49, 2

We are destined to die, and we do everything we can to avoid death. We cannot say the same for our efforts to avoid sin, despite the fact that we are called to eternal life. We're so attached to earthly things, and so little to heavenly goods, that we meticulously measure life in terms of seconds, minutes, hours, days, weeks, months, and years, often relegating our life in eternity to the back of our minds. We prepare ourselves spectacularly for a short trip, but how are we organizing our timeless final voyage?

Virtually everyone fears the death of the body, so few the death of the soul. Everyone worries about the death of the body, which must happen sooner or later, and does everything possible to avert it. . . . Yet all that one does to avoid death is in vain: at best one can only delay it, but never escape it. If instead one strives to avoid sin, he will not grow weary, and he will live forever.

Oh, if we could only succeed in urging others—and ourselves together with them—to love eternal life at least as much as they love fleeting life! What will a man not do when faced with the danger of death? How many, under threats hanging over their heads, have preferred to lose everything in order to save their lives! And who would not do so to avoid being struck down? And perhaps, even after having lost everything, some still lost their lives. Who would not be willing to give up the necessities of life just to stay alive, preferring a life of begging to an early death? If a man were told, "If you do not wish to die, you must sail the seas," would he even hesitate to do so? If a man were told, "If you do not wish to die, you must work," would he let himself be overcome by laziness? God commands us to do less burdensome things to give us eternal life, yet we neglect to obey.

THURSDAY

Gregory the Great, *Commentary on Job*, 21, 30

Humility helps us to recognize our need for the help of God and neighbor. Yes, we too, who think we know everything and can do anything on our own, must embrace our limits and see our lack. In this way, humility also helps us to see Christ himself—and not just an anonymous recipient of kindness—in the person we aid, awaiting our embrace.

One who puts on airs of importance in helping his neighbor commits the inner sin of pride, which wins out in proportion over the merit of the good external work. He remains naked inside while disdaining the naked person whom he clothes, and becomes worse than before by believing himself better than his neighbor in need. Indeed, one without humility is poorer than one without clothes. For this reason, when we observe the external destitution of our neighbors, we must reflect on the immensity of our own inner destitution; thus, we will not become inflated with a sense of superiority over them, plainly seeing how on the inside we are really more destitute than they.

FRIDAY

Origen, *Prayer*, 33, 1

Praying is stretching a hand toward the Infinite! It is a loving dialogue between our own impoverishment and the greatness of God. Our meager words, silence, abandonment, and meditation rise and go to the heavens. God will never hold back his hand when we turn to him with a sincere heart, with our limitations, and with our journey of faith.

At the beginning, when starting to pray, we must lift our praises to God with all our strength, through Christ, glorified in the Holy Spirit, who is with him. After this, general thanks will follow, thinking of the benefits bestowed on many people and the personal ones received from God. After this thanksgiving, I think that each person should seriously accuse his own sins before God, entreating him to save us and free us from the state to which those sins have led us, and to forgive us for the wrongs committed. After the confession of sins, sublime and heavenly gifts, both individual and collective, will be requested for relatives and friends. And prayer must ring out in all of this as continual praise of God, through Christ, in the Holy Spirit.

SATURDAY

John Chrysostom, *Homilies on Genesis*, 10

When we talk about fasting or abstinence, we risk falling into an exaggerated and unfruitful pietism linked to abstaining from meat on Fridays and fasting on Ash Wednesday and Good Friday. Not that these things should not be respected or taken into consideration, but they should be done with a sense of understanding and a free heart.

A men, amen, many are the ways that can open to us the gates of trust in the Lord: many more than simple fasting! Therefore, may he who eats but cannot fast prove himself through more generous almsgiving, fervent prayer, and readiness in listening to the divine Word: the weakness of the body is no obstacle to all of these things. And may he reconcile with his enemies and eradicate every feeling of revenge from his soul. If he does this, he observes the true fast that the Lord asks of us above all, because the purpose for which he commands us to refrain from eating is this: to quell the petulance of the flesh, making it docile to the fulfillment of the law of God.

FIRST WEEK OF LENT

SUNDAY

Jerome, *Letters (to Eustachius)*, I, 22, 37

There is a risk that fasting can turn into a sort of tightening noose that has nothing to do with Lent, which instead requires us to be free and willing. What sense does it make to fast on required days but eat immoderately on the days before and after? And for those who almost never eat meat for reasons of personal choice, what sacrifice would it be to abstain from it on Fridays? Fasting and abstinence should be rooted in meditation on the Word of God and in the heart.

I f you have fasted for two days, do not for this reason think yourself better than those who have not. You fast and perhaps become angry; another eats, but perhaps exercises kindness. You vent the frustration of your spirit and the hunger in your stomach in altercations; he, instead, eats in moderation and gives thanks to God. For this reason Isaiah cries out each day, "Is this the manner of fasting I wish . . . ?" (Is 58:5). Indeed, "you carry out your own pursuits, / and drive all your laborers. / Yes, your fast ends in quarreling and fighting, / striking with wicked claw. / . . . Do you call this a fast, / a day acceptable to the LORD?" (Is 58:3-5). What kind of fasting do you expect it to be if it leaves anger unchecked not just for one whole night, but for an entire month or longer? When you reflect on yourself, do not base your glory on the failings of others, but on the true value of your actions.

MONDAY

Augustine, *Sermons*, 311

We don't really know what to ask, and we fumble about looking for what really makes us happy. Oftentimes, we also pray poorly, quickly, distractedly, and without meditating. Following the lessons of Christ, and with the grace of the Holy Spirit, we can live Lent as a "school" for learning how to pray, asking for spiritual goods, and having a true encounter with God.

My child, why do you rise every day, pray, bend your knees, strike your forehead to the ground, and sometimes even cry while repeatedly imploring me: "My Father, my God, grant me a little wealth"? If I gave it to you, you would think you obtained something good and wonderful. You asked me for it and you received it: use it well. Before you had it, you were humble: now you are wealthier, and you disdain the poor. What good is it, if you have become worse? You were wicked and did not know what would make you worse: for this reason you asked it of me. I gave it to you, and I tested you: you found it, and what you were became clear. It was unknown when you did not have it. Correct yourself! Vomit your covetousness, and drink of charity. . . . But you ask me, "Is gold not good, then?" Certainly, gold is good. But the wicked will act wickedly with gold that is good; the upright act rightly with gold that is good. Thus you have seen those to whom I have said, "Ask me for something better, ask me for something more: ask me for me."

TUESDAY

Basil the Great, *Homily on Fasting*, 8

It's the period of Lent and the time of preparation for the central event of Christianity: Easter! Yes, preparation, as when preparing for an important party or meeting. We need to infuse it with that same passion, dedication, attention, and desire—but clearly in this case multiplying it all for God! Lent is, therefore, an excellent occasion, made up of forty intense days, for living with a focus on prayer, fasting, and good works. Difficult? Certainly not "easy," but why not think of it as "pleasing"?

Fasting is an occasion for joy. Indeed, just as thirst makes a drink sweeter and hunger makes a meal more appetizing, so fasting seasons the pleasure of eating. It sets itself squarely in the middle, interrupting the continuity of the pleasure of eating, thereby making the food seem more desirable and flavorful. For this reason, if you wish to prepare a delicious meal, prepare for it with fasting. But if you overindulge, you unknowingly render it insipid; for, by giving into an excess of appetite for a flavor, you suppress that flavor. Indeed, nothing is so desirable that it will not become nauseating after continually eating it. But that which we rarely taste, we eagerly enjoy. Thus, he who created us saw to it that his gifts would always be appreciated because of their constant changing throughout life. Do you not see how the sun is more radiant after the night? That waking is more serene after sleeping? And that health is more greatly appreciated after its opposite has been experienced? So a meal is more delightful after fasting: both for the wealthy who eat well, and for those whose fare is simple and frugal.

WEDNESDAY

Leo the Great, *Sermon 21, 3*

It's nice to feel loved in spite of ourselves and in spite of everything. God loves us above all things, and his embrace is all-encompassing. Feeling loved stirs up love; it is an awareness that calls each of us to recognize the uniqueness of every person, to rediscover our dignity, and to acknowledge the need for daily conversion.

O dearly beloved, let us therefore thank God the Father, through his Son, in the Holy Spirit. By means of the great love with which he loved us, he had mercy on us; and since we had died in sin, he gave us life back in Christ, so that in him we would be a new creation and a new work of his hands. Let us strip off the old man and his ways of action; and, given that we have been admitted to participate in the family of Christ, let us renounce the works of the flesh. Become aware, O Christian, of your dignity; and, having been made a participant in the divine nature, do not return to your prior baseness through behavior unworthy of your family. Remember who your head is, and of whose body you are a member. Recall that you were stripped away from the power of the shadows and carried into the light of the Kingdom of God. The Sacrament of Baptism has made you a temple of the Holy Spirit: do not cause such a great guest to flee because of your poor conduct; do not put yourself again into the slavery of the devil, for the price by which you were ransomed is the blood of Christ. He ransomed you out of mercy, but he will judge you in the truth of he who reigns with the Father and the Holy Spirit forever and ever. Amen.

Thursday

Theophilus of Alexandria, *Easter Letter (AD 401)*, 1

Preparing for Easter means preparing for a great feast, the most important one of the liturgical year. Joy becomes the adornment of our hearts, which reach out toward the divine while resting on earth. Good habits must be ready to go for the feast. May all of our thoughts be on God; may spiritual readings and prayer be light for our journey during these days.

Dearest brothers, let us unite our voices once again to praise Christ Jesus, the Lord of Glory, and let us eagerly respond to the invitation of the prophet, who says, "Sing to the LORD a new song" (Is 42:10). May those of us who share in the faith that leads to the Kingdom of Heaven joyously welcome and celebrate the upcoming feasts, which the entire world celebrates along with us. The invitation has been sent in a loud voice by one of the wise men: "Go, eat your bread with joy and drink your wine with a merry heart, because it is now that God favors your works" (Eccl 9:7). Indeed, those who do good, and who have ceased feeding on the milk of their youth to nourish themselves on more solid food, have a more profound understanding of things divine. Sated by this spiritual nourishment, they have God himself, who approves and gives witness to their lives. The author of Ecclesiastes addresses the following words to these table companions: "At all times let your garments be white, and spare not the perfume for your head" (Eccl 9:8). This is so that, dressed with virtue, they might imitate the radiance of the sun, pour oil over their intellect through the daily reading of Sacred Scripture, and prepare the lamp of their conscience so that, in accordance with the Gospel, it may shine for everyone in the home.

FRIDAY

Diadochus of Photike, *A Hundred Chapters on Spiritual Perfection*, 42

Lent offers us the occasion to gauge ourselves on the wholeness of the human person, giving us the occasion to integrate body and soul through prayer, fasting, and almsgiving. If we do not demand and seek a healthy internal and external balance in our faith journey, we run the risk of becoming "whitewashed tombs" (Mt 23:27): men and women who aim for the minimum and don't want to take flight.

Self-mastery is the common denominator of all the virtues; those who seek self-mastery must be masters of themselves in all things. Just as the amputation of any member of the human body disfigures the whole person, even if the missing part is scarcely significant, likewise a man who ignores a single virtue ruins—and how can he not know it?—all of the beauty of self-mastery. It is therefore necessary to take to heart not just the virtues regarding the body, but also those that can purify our inner self. What advantage will a man gain, for example, in keeping his body virgin but allowing his soul to be seduced by the demon of disobedience? Or, rather, how is it possible to crown a man who refrains from gluttony and every bodily appetite but has not taken care to control his conceit and craving for glory, or tolerated even a short-lived affliction—since the divine scale will give as recompense the light of justice, in accordance with their merits, to those who have carried out the works of justice with a spirit of humility?

SATURDAY

John Chrysostom, *Discourse II: Concerning Lazarus*

Math has never been my favorite subject, and I have always struggled to understand it, many times without success. With Christ, all of the diagrams and formulas go out the window, and I am happily confused. I certainly do not understand everything, but I like to reflect particularly on these points: my goods are not my own, but the Lord's; the more I have, the more I have to give; and if I keep everything for myself, I will be left with nothing. I'd say that settling accounts with Christ's method is a great way to overcome our limitations in math, and in many other areas.

Our goods belong to the Lord, regardless of their origin: and if we are generous toward the poor with them, we will receive in great abundance. If the Lord has allowed you to have more than others, it is not so that you can waste it in licentiousness, debauchery, gluttony, luxurious attire, or other comforts, but so that you can share it with those in need. If a public administrator has been entrusted with a portion of the king's money, and he neglects to distribute it to those to whom it was pledged in order to use it instead for his own pleasures, he will pay the penalty for it and bring about his own ruin. In the same way, a rich person is like an administrator who receives money for distribution to the poor, who has the charge of sharing it with his fellow servants in need.

Second Week
of Lent

Sunday

Hermas, *The Shepherd*, Similitude V

Fasting can even be easy, but sticking your neck out in solidarity and taking time away from other things are definitely the proving grounds. Certainly not everyone can go on missions or volunteer projects, but all of us know at least one person who might need care, attention, a ready smile, and a kind word. Charity can begin in the home, on the steps, down the sidewalk, at school, on campus, at work, or with friends.

I wish to teach you what type of fasting is complete and acceptable to the Lord. Listen to me. God does not want pointless fasting: offering such fasting to God does nothing for your holiness. You must offer a different kind of fasting to God, which is this: do nothing wicked in your life, but serve with Lord with a pure heart; obey his commandments and progress in his precepts; allow no evil desire to enter your soul, but trust in God. If you do this, if you have fear of God in this way, you will remain far away from all unrighteous works and you will live in God. If you do this, your fasting will be great and acceptable to the Lord.

Monday

Dorotheus of Gaza, *Directions on the Spiritual Life*, XV, 160

Hope entered the world with the Incarnation of Christ: that hope which "does not disappoint" (Rm 5:5), which turns the gravest sin into an occasion for repentance and redemption, which gives us the daily and constant opportunity for salvation in the Sacraments of Reconciliation and the Eucharist, and which during Lent each year renews our desire to participate anew in the Resurrection so that we can celebrate in the Father's house.

S o it is, brothers, that he who preserves himself rightly and well during these holy days is blessed; indeed, even if it should happen—given the human condition—that a man sin out of weakness or negligence, behold that God has granted him these holy days: if he endeavors to reflect on himself with vigilance and humility and to repent during this period, he is purified of the entire year's sins, his soul is relieved of their weight, and thus, in purity, he draws closer to the blessed day of the resurrection and can participate, without incurring judgment, in the holy mysteries. Through the penance of these holy fasts, he has become a new man and continues to celebrate with God in spiritual joy and delight.

TUESDAY

Augustine, *Tractates on the Gospel of St. John*, 14

Iron is tempered with fire, vases are hardened in ovens, children learn to walk after many falls, and a race is best run after strenuous physical preparation. So it is with faith, which is a gift that can take root and grow in the field of hope and self-abandonment, of self-sacrifice and self-offering, amid joy and suffering, through remembrance and witness.

The drops that fill rivers are tiny; grains of sand are tiny, but if there are many, their weight becomes crushing. A tiny leak in the hold of the boat, if neglected, allows water to enter little by little, producing the same effect as a single flooding wave: continuing to enter little by little, without ever being emptied, it sinks the boat. And what does this emptying mean, if not carrying out good works—mourning, fasting, almsgiving, forgiving—in order to avoid being drowned in sins? The journey in this life is difficult and fraught with trials: when things are going well, we should not boast; when things are going poorly, we should not lose heart. The happiness that the Lord concedes you in this life is to console you, not to corrupt you. And if he strikes you, he does so to correct you, not to lose you. Accept the correcting father if you do not wish to put the punishing judge to the test. These are things that we tell one another every day, and they should be repeated often because they are good and serve their purpose well.

WEDNESDAY

John Cassian, *Conferences*, 21, 5

We struggle against sin, and we should do so with strength in virtue of a sure ally: Jesus Christ. Sin is defeated with love, which is the essence of the Cross; with love of neighbor, which is the heart of the Gospel message; with heartfelt tears, but without self-pity; and with confession as the sacrament of God's love.

The complete and perfect definition of repentance requires that we permanently reject the sins for which we do penance or for which our conscience pricks us. It is then a sign that we have attained indulgence and satisfaction if we are able to strip away from our hearts any inner attachment to those sins. . . . Aside from the great, universal grace of Baptism and the most precious gift of martyrdom, which erases all guilt through the ablution of blood, there are still many other fruits of true repentance through which the expiation of sins may be attained. Indeed, eternal salvation is not promised only for penance aimed at the expiation of sins. . . . But love also knocks down a great number of sins. . . . Likewise, almsgiving also provides healing for our wounds. . . . So it is that tears shed obtain the cleansing of sins. . . . Purification is also granted through the confession of misdeeds.

Thursday

Gregory of Nazianzus, *On the Love for the Poor*, 26-29

Loving means taking care of others, finding common ground, being the first to notice when unhappiness arises or when suffering increases; noticing and being there, leaving behind our comforts that will surely await us. It's easy to think that others will be the ones to take care of the "least" on the streets or in hospitals, nursing homes, orphanages, and immigrant shelters. It is time for us to get working!

Whoever sails is never far from shipwrecking, and the more audaciously he sails, the closer it becomes. Whoever bears this body is never far from physical suffering, and the more he plows forward without consideration of those lying before him, the closer it becomes. So long as you are sailing with favorable winds, give a hand to those who are shipwrecked; so long as you are healthy and wealthy, help those who are suffering! Do not wait to experience for yourself how wretched it is to be inhuman, and how good it is to open your heart toward those in need. Do not wish to become an example of how God shows the strength of his arm against the proud, against those who pass by without taking care of the poor. Learn this from the calamities of others: give even just a little to those who are in need; it is not so little for those who need everything, and neither is it little to God, if it is in accordance with your means. Instead of a large sum of money, give your whole heart.

Friday

Augustine, *Tractates on the Gospel of St. John*, 73, 3-4

In his novel *The Last Crusader* (1956), Louis De Wohl writes the following: "Praying for something or someone is a very, very dangerous endeavor. You are always heard. And no one ever really knows what they're asking. I would never ask anything without adding 'If it's your will,' 'If it's for my good,' or something similar. Of course, sometimes God says 'no' to our prayers . . . Or so it seems. When he does so, his 'no' somehow turns into a flood of graces for someone else, and often for many others" (translated from Italian edition).

Therefore, when we wish the Lord to grant our prayers, let us ask him not in any way, but in his name: in the name of the Savior. And let us not ask anything that is an impediment to our salvation. . . . For those who believe in him, then, whatever they ask in his name—in the name that those who believe in him acknowledge as his—will be granted, because in this act he will be fulfilling his role as Savior. But if, out of ignorance, those who believe in him instead ask for something harmful to their salvation, they are not asking in the name of the Savior: the Lord would not be their Savior if he bestowed on them something unhelpful to their eternal salvation. In this case, therefore, it is much better for the believer if the Lord does not grant what has been asked: thus, he proves himself truly to be the Savior. This is the reason why the Savior, who is also the Good Teacher, teaches us what we should ask in the very prayer that he gave us: so that he may grant everything we ask.

SATURDAY

John Chrysostom, *Homilies on Genesis*, 10

"Physical fasting—for a certain period considered no longer fashionable—today appears to all as necessary. It is not difficult to understand that we should fast. Moreover, we find ourselves at times facing certain exaggerated forms that are due to a mistaken ideal of beauty. But physical fasting is important in every case because we are body and soul. The discipline of the body, material discipline too, is important for the spiritual life, which is always a life incarnate in a person who is both body and soul" (Pope Benedict XVI, Meeting with the Parish Priests and Clergy of the Diocese of Rome, February 7, 2008, *www.vatican.va*).

It is not wrong—how could it be!—to eat, but gluttony is harmful: filling your stomach beyond what is necessary, to the point that it seems to burst. This ruins the very pleasure of the food. Likewise, it is not wrong to drink wine in moderation, but it is wrong to abandon yourself to drunkenness and allow intemperance to disrupt your judgment and reason. If, because of your weakness, dear brother, you cannot maintain the fast for the whole day, anyone intelligent will not reproach you for it. Our Lord, then, who is gentle and loving and never asks of us anything we cannot handle, does not ask us to abstain from food and fast for ourselves, or simply to deprive us of food, but so that we will relinquish our daily concerns and fully commit ourselves to spiritual things.

THIRD WEEK
OF LENT

SUNDAY

Paulinus of Nola, *Poem 19*, 718-730

There are not too many words to be said at the foot of the Cross, just contemplation and mystery, just a crying mother and a faithful disciple. Yet in that moment, several words changed the course of history, and what seemed lost was found and renewed: the mother who no longer had her child remained a Mother, and a child received the gift of a Mother: a Mother for many children, the fruit of the marvelous Cross.

O Cross, wonderful goodness of God; Cross, glory of the heavens; Cross, eternal salvation of man; Cross, terror of the wicked, strength of the just, light of the faithful. O Cross, which allowed God in flesh to become the salvation of the earth and man to reign over God in the heavens. The light of truth shined for you, and the cruel night fled.

You destroyed the temples with shaken foundations for the converted pagans; you, harmonious buckle of peace, who reconciled man through the covenant of Christ.

You are the ladder by which man can be brought into heaven. Be always pillar and anchor for us, your faithful devotees, that our house may be solid and our ships safe.

Set your faith on the Cross, and from the Cross receive your crown.

Monday

John Chrysostom, *Homilies on the Gospel of Matthew*, 54, 4-5

Do you adore the man who was crucified? St. John Chrysostom invites us in this passage to proclaim our faith with clarity and joy, to praise the splendor of spiritual goods obtained from it, and to unceasingly adore it as the means and symbol of the salvation of our souls. Through the Cross, he says, "dying is no longer death, but sleep." Let us embrace it with open hearts!

I mpress this sign upon your heart, therefore, and embrace this Cross to which we owe the salvation of our souls. It is indeed the Cross that has saved and converted the entire world, banished error, reestablished truth, made the earth into heaven, and made men into angels. Thanks to the Cross, demons have ceased to be so much cause for fear and have become detestable, and dying is no longer death, but sleep. Through the Cross, everything that fought against us has been knocked to the ground and trampled over. So if someone asks you whether you adore the man who was crucified, respond with a clear voice and a joyful mien: "Yes, I adore him, and I will never cease adoring him."

TUESDAY

Cyril of Jerusalem, *Catechetical Lectures XVIII*, 20

Who knows me better than you, Lord? All the hairs of my head are counted, every star is called by name. "You have probed me, you know me" (Ps 139:1), you want what's best for me, but you want me to get there through awareness and sacrifice, urging me to choose the good, in virtue of an inheritance that will never diminish.

We will be held accountable to the Lord for all the things we have done. Man is often not aware, but the Creator is an honest witness, remaining faithful in heaven and observing all that happens. The stains of sin remain in the body. Just as a bodily wound leaves a scar even after it has healed, so do sins wound the soul and the body, and the scarred signs remain in everyone. They are erased only in those who receive purification. God heals the old wounds of the soul and of the body through Baptism. Together, may we all fore-arm ourselves to preserve the purity of our bodily vestment and to not lose hold of reality—of heavenly salvation—through vile fornication or a lascivious act or some other sin, but to inherit the eternal Kingdom of God, from which he makes you all worthy through his grace.

WEDNESDAY

Dorotheus of Gaza, *Directions on the Spiritual Life*, XVI, 172

What we are is the fruit of the love of God, who sent his only Son into the world for us. Dying and rising for the salvation of all, he has given us an incredible gift that extends from the arms of the Cross to the ends of the earth. Looking to the Cross, what we will become depends on us: on whether we want to live as free men and women or as slaves to sin.

We are conscious of the sense of mystery and for whom Christ died. The sense of mystery in the Death of Christ is this: after we destroyed our conformity to the image of God through sin, and were therefore dead . . . , that God who had made us in his image took pity on his creature and on his image, made himself man for us, and accepted death for us, in order to lead us dead people back to the life which we had lost through our transgression. He ascended his holy Cross himself and crucified sin, by which we had been driven out of paradise, and, as it is written, he took captivity captive (see Eph 4:8). . . . Therefore, ascending high upon the holy and life-giving Cross, Christ freed us with his own blood from the captivity in which the enemy held us because of that transgression. . . . We were thus freed from hell through the love of Christ for us. Now it is up to us to go to heaven, because the enemy no longer commands us as before, and we are no longer his slaves.

THURSDAY

Chromatius of Aquileia, *Sermon 15, 4*

There is no moment of the Passion of Christ that is not linked by the single, red thread of his boundless love for us! His words and deeds are striking, direct, incisive, and shocking: all for our salvation. Those who had everything are left with nothing, and he has given his everything in exchange for our nothing. Accept, O Lord, the little that I am, set before the everything that you are.

The Lord took off his tunic and wrapped himself in a towel; he poured water into a basin and began to wash the feet of his disciples, drying them with the towel around his waist. It was not recounted without reason that the Lord removed his tunic and thus washed the feet of his disciples. In no other moment were the feet of our souls washed and the steps of our spirit purified than when the Lord stripped himself of his tunic; then, on the Cross, he truly laid down the tunic of his flesh, which he had donned at the moment of his birth and of which he stripped himself during the Passion. And it was in order to cover up our nakedness that he stripped himself of the tunic of his flesh. And thus, this tunic alone of the body of Christ was enough to clothe the entire world. And though the Lord had stripped himself of the tunic of his flesh through the Passion, he did not remain naked, for he had the garments of his virtues.

FRIDAY

Hermas, *The Shepherd*, Mandate IX

The disciples asked Jesus, "Lord, teach us to pray" (Lk 11:1). They asked him to teach them to pray just as he, though he was God, prayed to the Father. He then taught how, where, and in what manner to pray: "This is how you are to pray: Our Father" (Mt 6:9); "when you pray, go to your inner room, close the door, and pray to your Father in secret" (Mt 6:6), and "do not babble" (Mt 6:7). God knows what we need!

Push every doubt away and do not hesitate, even for an instant, to ask the Lord for a grace, thinking to yourself: "How is it possible for me to ask and receive from the Lord, since I have sinned so much against him?" Do not think this, but turn to him with your whole heart and pray to him without faltering; you will experience his great mercy. God is not like men, who hold grudges; he forgets offences and has pity on his creature. Therefore, first purify your heart of the vanities of this world and of all the sins we have mentioned, then pray to the Lord and you will receive everything. Your every prayer will be granted if you ask without hesitation. . . . If it then happens that you ask the Lord for a grace and he delays in granting it, do not allow yourself to become discouraged for not having immediately received what you requested: this delay in receiving the requested grace is surely either a test or due to an unknown wrong you have committed. Therefore, do not cease addressing your private request to God, and it will be granted.

SATURDAY

John Chrysostom, *Homilies on Genesis*, 10

Fasting is a balanced choice; in fact, it provides strength to those who recognize their earthly weaknesses through faith and humility, and it helps them become steadfast, shifting them toward spiritual things. Human beings naturally tend toward the search for "something more," for overabundance, and they often set aside what is truly important and essential. Fasting during Lent can be the opportunity for each of us to reestablish a hierarchy of values.

I f we guided our lives with a commitment to sobriety, applied all of our energy to spiritual things, ate only as much food as required by absolute necessity, and committed our lives to good works, we would not need to strengthen ourselves by fasting. But since human nature is indolent and readily abandons itself to distractions and pleasures, our good Lord—like a loving father—gave us the medicine of fasting, so that these pleasures could be taken away and we could be driven to shift our attention from the everyday necessities of life to spiritual works. Hence, if a man cannot fast due to physical weakness, he should not deprive himself of food; I urge him to treat his infirmity. But not for this reason should he deprive himself of spiritual teachings; indeed, he should apply himself with even greater effort.

Fourth Week
of Lent

Sunday

Lactantius, *Epitome of the Divine Institutes*, 67

Recognizing that we are sinners is an act of great humility, the first step toward conversion, and the first rung on the ladder of salvation. It was in this way that the prodigal son realized his mistake and returned to his father's house, ready to be the least of his servants; but what amazement at finding himself met, embraced, and celebrated by his merciful father!

Our fragile nature does not allow anyone to be without blemish. So it is that our best remedy is to take refuge in repentance, which holds an important place among the virtues since it is self-improvement: thus, if we fall either in word or in deed, we immediately mend our ways, confess that we have sinned, and ask for forgiveness from God, who in his mercy does not deny it unless we persist in our error. The help of penance is great; its consolation is abundant. It is healing from the wounds of sin; it is hope, the harbor of salvation. He who denies it takes away that which gives life to one's life, because no one can be so upright that penitence is not at times necessary. But even if we have not sinned, we must nonetheless open our souls to God and implore him all the same because of our failings, thanking him even in the midst of adversity.

Monday

Ambrose, *Commentary on the Gospel of St. Luke*, 10, 88-90

Crying is not a sign of weakness as long as we are not whiners; crying is not a defeat as long as it does not turn into a habitual way of reacting and communicating; crying is not harmful even though it does physical harm. Mary cried for her only son on the Cross; the women who met Christ along the way of the Cross cried, and so did their children. May our tears be purification for a new life, may they be the result of sincere and genuine emotions as we find ourselves before the boundless love pouring from the Cross, as we are watched from the Cross with love by he who cried, though he was God himself.

Peter became saddened and cried because he erred like all men. I cannot find what he said; I find only that he cried. I read his tears, I do not read what he gave in recompense; but what cannot be excused can be cleansed. . . . Tears speak of the offence without horrifying; tears recognize the sin without causing one to blush; tears do not ask forgiveness, but they merit it. I discovered why Peter remained silent: so that, asking for forgiveness so quickly, he would not further increase his guilt. First we must cry, then we must pray. Excellent tears, so that they cleanse the guilt. Indeed, those who see Christ's gaze begin to cry. Peter denied him a first time but did not shed a tear, because the Lord's gaze did not meet his; he denied him a second time and did not shed a tear, because the Lord's gaze had not yet come upon him; he denied him a third time, Christ's gaze fell upon him, and he cried bitterly. Gaze upon us, Lord Jesus, so that we may learn to cry for our sins.

Tuesday

Cyril of Jerusalem, *Catechetical Lectures IV*, 14

The Cross points above, and we were made for heaven. Christ ascended into heaven through the way of the Cross. He indicates the road and gives us the correct coordinates: "in the name of the Father, and of the Son, and of the Holy Spirit." The Sign of the Cross is the daily and constant meeting point between our poorness and the magnificence of God.

L et us not be ashamed of the Cross of Christ, but rather, even if another makes the Sign of the Cross inconspicuously, teach him to do so in front of everyone so the demons, seeing that regal sign, will take flight in trembling. Make the Sign of the Cross when you eat and drink, when you sit or lie down, when you rise, when you speak, when you walk: in any situation. Indeed, he who was crucified down here is now in heaven on high. Of course, if he had remained in the tomb after being crucified and buried, then we would certainly have reason to be ashamed! Instead, the man who was crucified on this Golgotha ascended into heaven from the Mount of Olives in the East. Indeed, after having descended from the earth into hell, and having returned from there to us, he rose yet again from our world into heaven, while the Father, hailing him, addressed him with these words: "Take your throne at my right hand, / while I make your enemies your footstool" (Ps 110:1).

WEDNESDAY

Augustine, *Sermons*, 254, 4-5

The liturgical periods of Lent and the Easter season are propitious moments to reflect on God's love for us, on faith as a gift, on the mystery of life and death, on the eschatological perspective, and on salvation in Christ. They are times that allow us to foretaste and desire what we will one day be, but also to joyfully sing for our "here and now."

This, our current time of destitution and tears, is symbolized by the forty days before Easter; the time to follow—a time of gladness, peace, happiness, eternal life, and endless reigning that has yet to come—is instead symbolized by the fifty days during which we lift up our praises to God. In other words, we are presented with two time periods: one before the Resurrection of the Lord, and the other after the Resurrection of the Lord. One is the time in which we now live, the other is the time in which we one day hope to live. The present time of weeping, symbolized by the forty days of Lent, is the time in which we live and which we symbolize in ourselves; the time of joy, peace, and reigning, symbolized by the days of the Pentecost, is expressed by our alleluia, though we do not yet truly possess these praises. But for now, we pine for the alleluia. What does "alleluia" mean? "Praise God." But we do not yet possess these praises: the praises of God after the Resurrection re-echo in the Church, because our own praising will be eternal only after our resurrection.

Thursday

John Cassian, *Conferences*, 21, 14-15

"Take care not to perform righteous deeds in order that people may see them; otherwise, you will have no recompense from your heavenly Father. When you give alms, do not blow a trumpet before you, as the hypocrites do in the synagogues and in the streets to win the praise of others. Amen, I say to you, they have received their reward. But when you give alms, do not let your left hand know what your right is doing, so that your almsgiving may be secret. And your Father who sees in secret will repay you" (Mt 6:1-4).

Fasting is dangerous for those who use it to seek human praise and who acquire a saintly reputation by showing their vain pallor; the Gospel words tell us that they have already received their recompense in this life. . . . Therefore, take note of how the Lord does not consider fasting a primary good: it is not pleasing to God in itself, but in merit of the other good works it brings with it. . . . Mercy, patience, and charity, the norms of the afore-mentioned virtues that are the primary good, should not be practiced for fasting, but rather fasting should be practiced for them. Indeed, one should work to acquire these truly good virtues through the practice of fasting, and not simply employ them to achieve fasting as their final goal. Bodily suffering is helpful to them, so the tool of hunger should be applied to assist us in achieving charity, the eternal good that is immutable and free from all temporal restrictions.

Friday

Origen, *Prayer*, 31, 2-4

In order to pray well, we must free our hearts and create silence around and within ourselves. We often think that gushing rivers of words is the best way to pray, but perhaps it's just a way of reassuring ourselves. Christ teaches us that prayer is a relationship: it is intimacy and depth in relation to God. More than opening our mouths too much, we should open our hearts to the grace of God and ask forgiveness!

I am convinced that one who stops for a moment and settles himself before praying will be more fervent and collected throughout his time of prayer. Likewise for one who distances himself from all concerns and perturbing thoughts, calling to mind with all of his strength the grandeur he is approaching and how impious it would be to present himself emptily and distractedly—I would almost say disparagingly. When going to pray, one should set aside every other thought and set his soul in his hands, almost tangibly guiding his mind to God, and before putting himself in the appropriate position—raising the highest part of his soul toward the presence of the Lord of all—he should distance his thoughts from offenses against him, just as each of us does not wish God to remember our own wicked actions, our many sins committed against our neighbor, and all the actions contrary to right reason that we are each aware of having committed.

SATURDAY

Leo the Great, *Oration 55*, 3

"Today you will be with me in Paradise" (Lk 23:43). These words promising salvation to the thief, uttered by the crucified, pain-stricken Christ, are truly moving. We call him "the thief," and yet Christ looked at him with love and did not hesitate to make him the greatest of all promises. There has been no other man or woman to receive this solemn guarantee from Christ of living with him in Paradise. The fruits of salvation from the Cross begin right on the Cross.

The Cross of Christ is the sacrament of the true and prophetic altar on which, through the host of salvation, the offering of human nature is celebrated. It is here that the immaculate blood of the Lamb erased our condemnation from Original Sin, that the opposition by satanic tyranny was quashed, that humility triumphed over pride, and that the effects of faith were so rapid that, of the two thieves crucified with Christ, the one who believed in the Son of God was justified and entered Paradise. Who can explain the mystery of such a magnificent gift? Who will tell of the power of such a conversion? In an instant, the guilt of countless crimes passed through Christ, amid the tortures of his agony on that instrument of execution, and the grace of Christ gave a crown to a man who had been condemned for his wrong-doing.

Fifth Week of Lent

Sunday

Leo the Great, *Oration 60, 4-7*

The Cross is a wonderful manifestation of divine mercy. It is the assistant, the beginning, and the end of our Lenten journey with Christ toward salvation. The first step is always God's: his free and gratuitous gesture of love, rich with grace and mercy. For us, this means being loved as we are and where we are in our journey, abandoning ourselves to him with faith and joy.

Thus, when the Lord was carrying the wood of the Cross—wood that he later turned into a scepter of power—it seemed greatly degrading to the eyes of unbelievers, but it appeared as a wonderful mystery to believers, because the glorious victor over the devil and conqueror of the forces of hell was carrying the beautifully symbolic trophy of this triumph. And on his shoulders, with tireless patience, he displayed the sign of salvation so that all would adore it, almost as though he were trying to encourage all of his followers from that very moment. . . . O marvelous power of the Cross! O ineffable glory of the Passion! In it we find the tribunal of the Lord, the judgment of the world, and the kingdom of the Crucified.

Monday

Cyril of Jerusalem, *Catechetical Lectures XIII, 35-36*

The Sign of the Cross is the beginning and also the end of all our prayers. This simple yet rich gesture accompanies our awakening in the morning, our mealtimes at table, and the end of our day. It's the sign of blessing, an "efficacious aid" for all of us, which touches both heart and mind. Let's not allow it to become unappreciated or superstitious, and let's not make it hastily or hide it!

The wood of life was planted on earth so that, after being abhorred, it would become blessed and the dead would be freed. Let us not be ashamed, then, to profess the Crucified Christ. On any occasion, let us trace the Sign of the Cross with our fingers: when we eat bread or drink, when we enter or exit, before going to sleep, when we are lying down or when we rise, whether we are moving or sitting still. It is an efficacious aid that is free for the poor and effortless for the weak. In fact, it is a grace from God: the mark of believers and the terror of demons. Indeed, with this sign the Lord triumphed over them, exposing them to public derision. . . . Therefore do not disdain this sign, for the simple reason that it is a gift; rather, honor your benefactor all the more because of it.

TUESDAY

John Damascene, *An Exposition of the Orthodox Faith*, 4, 11

We remain in silence before the Cross for silent adoration, meditation on its mystery, or prayers of thanksgiving. In prayer, we travel the Way of the Cross as a community united around its Savior, who offered himself on the altar of the Cross, which is mystically and simultaneously the pathway to heaven, a reference point for our faith, a sign indicating the path of salvation, support for those who falter, and victory over evil.

However much every action or manifestation of Christ is magnificent, divine, and extraordinary, none of them is so worthy of admiration as the Cross, which is in itself worthy of all veneration. Nor in fact was death destroyed by anything other than the Cross of our Lord Jesus Christ. . . . Indeed, the Word on the Cross is considered the might of God, since his power and strength—his victory over death—has been manifested to us through it. Just as the four parts of the Cross hold together and are linked by their central point, so sublimity and depth are coupled by the power of God, forming that space in which every visible and invisible creature is contained. . . . It is raising-up for all those lying down, fulcrum for those who are standing, cane for the infirm, shepherd's staff for the sheep, aid for those who mend their ways, perfection for the departing, salvation of body and soul, rejection of evils, cause of all good things, destruction of sin, blueprint for the resurrection, and the wood of eternal life.

Wednesday

John Chrysostom, *Homilies on the Gospel of Matthew*, 54, 4-5

The Cross often continues to be a stumbling block (see 1 Cor 1:23) in today's secularist society. It remains incomprehensible to those who do not look to it with faith, becomes flamboyance for those who turn it into a fashionable symbol, and is misunderstood by Christians who make it a simple house decoration. And yet for many, the Cross is accepting an existence of suffering with hope, with the decision to give themselves to others; it is being Christian and being persecuted because of it; it is having the courage to give witness to God's love even to the ends of the earth.

Therefore let no one be ashamed of the sacred and venerable symbols of our salvation, of the Cross which is the summit and apex of all our goods, through which we live and are who we are. Let us carry the Cross of Christ everywhere, as a crown. Everything that affects us is carried out and fulfilled through it. When we need to be renewed by Baptism, the Cross is present; when we nourish ourselves on that mystical food which is the Body of Christ, when hands are laid upon us in consecration to the ministry of the Lord, or when we do anything else, this symbol of victory is always and everywhere alongside us, sustaining us. . . . The Cross is in fact the sign of our salvation and of the shared freedom of the human race, the sign of the mercy of the Lord, who allowed himself to be led like a sheep to the slaughter for love of us (see Is 53:7).

THURSDAY

Leo the Great, *Sermon 8*

May all of us give what we can to help those in need: whether it be a kind word, food, clothing, a hug, a smile, money, or our time. May all of us give according to our means, knowing that in our neighbor we find Christ: poor, sad, lonely, sick, weak, imprisoned, dirty, marginalized, jobless, or homeless.

Though all of our means may not be the same, our piety in giving should be. Indeed, the generosity of believers is not measured by the import of the gift, but by the benevolence involved. Therefore, even the poor should offer a contribution to this exchange of mercy, sacrificing something from their earnings—however meager—that will not cause them great sadness, in order to sustain those in need. The wealthy should give more abundantly, but the spirit of the poor should be no less generous. Indeed, as much as it is hoped to harvest more after planting more seed, it may be that a smaller number of seeds provide many more fruits of justice. Our judge is just and true and does not defraud anyone of the reward for his merits. He wants us to take care of the poor for this reason, so that as Christ our God determines our future recompense, he can pour out his promised mercy on those who are merciful.

FRIDAY

Cyprian, *On the Lord's Prayer*, 35-36

Life in eternal beatitude would be a constant prayer of praise to the Trinity. May our life in this world prepare us for what we will become in God's presence. Let us allow ourselves to be molded by our Creator through prayer, that he may give us shape, fashion us, and make us into an ever more accurate likeness of himself, so that we may one day be worthy of living in his presence forever.

When is he who has light in his heart deprived of light? When is it not sunny, when is it not daytime for those who have Christ as their sun and their day? . . . We, dearest brothers, who are always in the light of the Lord, who always recall and preserve what we have started to become by the gift of grace, consider the night to be day. In faith we believe that we always walk in the light, and never allow ourselves to be thwarted by the shadows from which we have fled. The nighttime hours cause no harm to our prayers; laziness and sloth never take us away from prayer. Spiritually renewed and reborn through the goodness of God, we imitate what we shall one day become. We will live in a kingdom where there will only be day, without the interruption of night; therefore, let us be vigilant at night as though it were day. We will constantly pray and give thanks to God; therefore, let us not cease praying and thanking him while we are down here, either.

SATURDAY

Basil the Great, *Homily on Fasting*, 1

"When you fast, do not look gloomy like the hypocrites. They neglect their appearance, so that they may appear to others to be fasting. Amen, I say to you, they have received their reward. But when you fast, anoint your head and wash your face, so that you may not appear to others to be fasting, except to your Father who is hidden. And your Father who sees what is hidden will repay you" (Mt 6:16-18).

L et us prepare ourselves, as we have been taught, for the feasts that draw nearer: not with sullen expressions, but with the joy that is becoming of saints. The dejected are not crowned; the weeping do not receive the trophy. Do not be sad while you are being cared for. It would be foolish not to rejoice in the health of your soul, instead lamenting about the sacrifice of food and thereby proving that you give more importance to pleasing your belly than to healing your soul. Satiety is a delight for the belly; fasting is a profit for the soul. Be glad that the doctor has given you a medicine capable of canceling sin! Like worms that germinate in the intestines of children and need to be driven out by the bitterest of medicine, so sins that abide in the depths of the soul are killed by fasting—provided it is truly worthy of being called such—as soon as it touches the soul.

Holy Week

Palm Sunday

Theophilus of Alexandria, *Easter Letter* (AD 404), 11

Escaping death is the desire of every person; accepting it and conquering it is possible for those who are brothers and sisters in Christ who conquered death. The invisible God became visible, and the blood he shed on the Cross testifies to it; we find a still greater testimony in the Resurrection, to which we will all one day be called.

The foolish believed that Christ, born of the Virgin, was only what he appeared to be in their eyes; but the wise discovered the invisible God beneath his works and the wonder of his miracles. It is true that his appearance is that of a man, but his power proves him to be God, hidden in the humiliating condition of a servant. And despite how the Jews imprisoned him and impiously shouted that he should be crucified—blaspheming God by putting his body to death, and indeed becoming slaves of impiousness by killing the flesh of the Lord—he nonetheless approached death courageously to offer us an example of fortitude. And as St. Peter says, he proved himself the Lord of Glory precisely during his Passion by remaining impassible in divine majesty though his body suffered. He bore this suffering for us, and that is why he did not escape death.

Monday of Holy Week

Gregory of Nazianzus, *On the Love for the Poor*, 36, 39-40

Charity is nothing other than love received and given in turn. It's enough to look around ourselves to see the needs of the world, of our cities, and of those who are alongside us. Many people, both near and far, are waiting for someone to bend toward them, for an outstretched hand to help them get back up. That hand can be mine or yours!

D o you think that love of neighbor is not a duty for you, but an option? That it is not a law, but a piece of advice? I also truly hoped so, and was convinced of it. But I am terrified by the left hand of the divine Judge, the goats, and his rebukes from his seat on the throne: they are judged and put at his left not because they stole, committed sacrilegious robberies or adulterous acts, or perpetrated some other forbidden act, but because they did not take care of Christ in those in need. Therefore, if you wish to listen to me, O servants of Christ, O my brothers and fellow heirs, let us visit Christ, care for Christ, feed Christ, clothe Christ, shelter Christ, and honor Christ while we still have time: not just at table, like some; not with precious oil like Mary; not just with the tomb like Joseph of Arimathea, nor with funeral ceremonies like Nicodemus, Christ's half-friend; nor with gold, frankincense, and myrrh like the wise men, as it is said. But since the Lord asks everyone for works of mercy and not sacrifice, and true goodness is greater than a thousand fat calves, we show him this by caring for those in need who lie prostrate on the ground this day.

Tuesday of Holy Week

Jerome, *Commentary on Psalm 96*

In Psalm 96, we read: "Let the heavens be glad and the earth rejoice; / let the sea and what fills it resound; / let the plains be joyful and all that is in them. / Then let all the trees of the forest rejoice / before the Lord who comes, / who comes to govern the earth, / to govern the world with justice / and the peoples with faithfulness" (11-13). Walking through the places where Jesus lived and silently praying is one of the most beautiful experiences a Christian can have, but it's even more meaningful to make our hearts a welcoming place where Christ can continue to walk today.

When I talk about the Cross, I'm not thinking of the wood, but of the suffering. . . . Happy is he who carries the Cross, the Resurrection, and the place of Christ's birth and Ascension in his heart! Happy is he who has Bethlehem in his heart, that is, who allows Christ to be reborn in his heart each day! What does "Bethlehem" mean, anyway? "House of bread." We are also a bread house: a house for the bread come down from heaven. Christ is nailed to the Cross each day for us. We are crucified to the world, and Christ is crucified within us. Happy is he in whose heart Christ rises every day, when he makes penance for even his most trifling sins. Happy is he who ascends each morning from the Mount of Olives to the Kingdom of Heaven, where the flourishing olive trees of the Lord grow, where the light of Christ overlooks, where the olive groves of the Lord are found.

WEDNESDAY OF HOLY WEEK

Lactantius, *Epitome of the Divine Institutes*, 51

"The Cross of Christ! Ever blossoming, the tree of the Cross continues to bear new fruits of salvation. This is why believers look with confidence to the Cross, drawing from its mystery of love the courage and strength to walk faithfully in the footsteps of the crucified and risen Christ. Thus the message of the Cross has entered the hearts of so many men and women and changed their lives" (Pope John Paul II, Homily for the Canonization of Edith Stein, October 11, 1998, *www.vatican.va*).

I know that many people distance themselves from the truth, because they abhor the very name of the Cross; and yet there is profound meaning and great power in it. He was sent to open wide the path of salvation to the humblest of men; thus he humbled himself to free them. He accepted the type of death usually reserved for the least of men, so that everyone might be able to imitate him. . . . In addition to this, he had to be raised because he accepted his Passion and Death. And the Cross raised him both symbolically and literally, so that his power and majesty might become evident by his Passion. Stretching out his arms on the wooden beam, he also spread his wings toward East and West, so that he might gather all people from every part of the world under them, bringing peace. The strength and power of this sign become clear, when by it all the ranks of demons are driven out and put to flight.

Holy Thursday

Cyrillona, *Hymn on the Washing of the Feet*

Humility fosters humility, the model gives rise to imitators, and witness urges service. "Whoever believes in me will do the works that I do, and will do greater ones than these" (Jn 14:12): this is Christ's promise to his disciples and to all those who follow him. It's shocking to think that we could do something even just equal to what he did, and unimaginable to think we could do greater things! And yet this has been promised by he who is the Witness par excellence, and the history of the Church throughout the world unwaveringly tells us of the fulfillment of that promise.

Our Lord guided the Twelve and led them home to wash their feet. He assigned them their role as heirs, and then rose to serve them as their friend. He poured the water of charity and carried the basin, took the towel and wrapped it around his waist. . . . "If I do not wash you, you will have no inheritance with me. If I do not wash you, return to me the keys I have entrusted to you. If I do not wash you, even your rule will be taken from you." If, as you ask, I do not wash you, you will not even be able to participate in my body. Then Simon Peter began to implore him, saying, "O Lord, do not wash only my feet, but my hands and head as well!" Jesus responded, "Simon, Simon, for the whole body there is only a bath in holy water!" He finished the work of washing their feet and commanded them out of love: "Look, my disciples, at how I have served you and at the work I have assigned you to do! Look at how I have washed and cleaned you; now hurry quickly to the church, and pass through its doors as heirs! Tread over demons without fear and on the head of the serpent without being frightened! Go on your way without fear and announce my word in the cities! Spread the Gospel to the nations and instill love in the hearts of all! Announce my Gospel before kings and witness to my faithfulness before judges! See that I who am your God have lowered myself and served you so that I could prepare a perfect Easter, and the face of the entire earth could rejoice!" [See Jn 13.]

GOOD FRIDAY

John Chrysostom, *Discourses on the Cross and the Thief*, I, 1, 4

Adoring the Cross means taking up part of its weight, being like the man from Cyrene who lightened Christ's burden on the path of suffering. Adoring the Cross means being aware that we are not alone in the struggle against sin, and that even the worst of thieves can reach heaven by looking to the Crucified Christ.

Today our Lord Jesus Christ is on the Cross, and we celebrate so that you understand how the Cross is an occasion of rejoicing and a spiritual celebration. The Cross did indicate disdain at first, but today the Cross is venerable; it was first a symbol of condemnation, but today it is hope for salvation. It has truly become the source of countless blessings; it has freed us from error, cleared away our shadows, reconciled us with God, transformed us from enemies of God into his family, and from strangers into his neighbors. This Cross is the destruction of enmity, the source of peace, and the chest for our treasure. Thanks to the Cross, we no longer wander in the desert, for we have found the right way; we are no longer outside the palace, for we have found the entrance; we no longer fear the flaming arrows of the devil, for we have seen where the font of water is. Thanks to the Cross there is no longer widowhood, for we have the Groom; we no longer fear wolves, for we have the Good Shepherd. Thanks to the Cross we no longer fear the tyrant, for we are by the side of the King.

Holy Saturday

Ambrose, *Commentary on the Gospel of St. Luke*, 10, 140ff.

We do not adore the empty tomb, but the Risen Christ! We set our gaze not on a silent tombstone, but on the tabernacle that guards him who is alive in the Eucharist; we do not celebrate on cold marble, but on the altar of his body and blood; we do not bring flowers that wilt, but good works that are a treasure in heaven.

And it is not without purpose that one Evangelist wrote that the tomb was empty, and another that it was the tomb of Joseph. Consequently, Christ did not have a tomb of his own. In effect, a tomb is prepared for those who are subject to the law of death; but the victor over death does not have his own tomb. What type of relationship could there be between a tomb and God? In fact, the Book of Ecclesiastes states the following regarding one who meditates upon the good: "He has no burial." Therefore, though death is shared by all, the Death of Christ is unique, and therefore he is not buried together with others, but is closed in a tomb by himself. Indeed, the Incarnation of the Lord had all of the characteristics typical of human birth, but the similarities went together with a difference in nature: he was born of the Virgin by a similar generation but a dissimilar conception. He healed the sick, but also reigned. John baptized with water; Christ baptized with the Spirit. The Death of Christ is therefore like all others in its bodily nature, but unique in its power.

EASTER VIGIL

Augustine, *Sermon Guelpherbytanus 5*

O blessed night, only you were given to know the time and the hour that Christ rose from hell. It was written that this night would shine like day, and become the source of light for your joy. The holy mystery of this night defeats evil, washes away guilt, and restores innocence to sinners and joy to the sorrowing. It dispels hatred, bends the rigidness of the powerful, and promotes harmony and peace. O truly glorious night, you reunite the earth with heaven, and men and women with their Creator! (See Exultet, Easter Vigil.)

It is understood, without a doubt, that this night exists in sight of the following day, which we call the Lord's. And, in any event, he had to rise during the night so that he could illuminate our shadows by his Resurrection. Nor was it in vain, in fact, that his people sang to him long before this night: "You, LORD, give light to my lamp; / my God brightens the darkness about me" (Ps 18:29). So it is that our devotion entrusts us to such a profound mystery: so that just as our faith is strengthened by his Resurrection and already remains vigilant, so may our vigil shine through this resplendent night; and so that with the Church spread throughout the world, we may be sure that we will not be found in the darkness of night.

For the many great peoples who gather everywhere around the world to celebrate this solemnity in the name of Christ, the sun may disappear but the day does not end, for the brilliant earth and dazzling sky take its place. Nonetheless, if anyone wishes to learn the reasons for such a marvelous vigil, he can easily find them and respond in faith. Without a doubt, he who granted us the glory of his name has brightened this night, and to him we say, "You brighten the darkness around me." Allow the light to open our eyes, so that we may look upon this splendor of light with radiant eyes, able to see the cause for such a brilliant night with unclouded minds.

Augustine, *Sermon Guelpherbytanus 5*

The Easter Vigil is the "mother of all vigils"! Keeping vigil means staying awake, ready, and alert; keeping vigil is preparing your heart for sacrifice with the certainty of receiving an incredible gift; keeping vigil is praying while abandoning yourself and the time that passes by; keeping vigil is renewing the experience of the tomb, which becomes empty by the Resurrection of Christ; keeping vigil is foretasting an endless vigil.

How wonderful, then, that Christians keep vigil today on the anniversary of this celebration! In fact, we now keep vigil to a high degree, and no other solemnity can compare. With this desire to keep watch, we wonder and ask ourselves, "For how many hours do we keep vigil?" We keep vigil for many days, as though the other vigils were not worthy of the name in comparison to this one. And even the Apostle recommended constancy in fasting and in keeping vigil when he reminded himself, "More frequent fasting and keeping vigil"; but the vigil of this night is so immense that it alone surpasses the name even of all the others combined, as if they were part of it. . . . Like life itself, so the vigil will become everlasting in the eternal realm; in that place, living will mean nothing other than keeping vigil, and keeping vigil will mean nothing other than living. . . . And for this reason, it is doubtless that whoever keeps vigil diligently, soberly, and innocently meditates on the life of angels: the more the weakness of the body weighs us down on this earth, the more our desires for heaven become suppressed. By keeping such a lengthy vigil against that weight which brings death, the prize of eternal life is prepared for us.

EASTER: RESURRECTION SUNDAY

John Chrysostom, *On the Resurrection*, 3-5

Jesus has freed us from sin and from the power of death. He has joined what was separated by Adam and Original Sin. He redeemed the corrupt world through his Death on the Cross, and he paid the ransom for us all through his Resurrection. He has reestablished the original order before handing everything over to the Father on the last day.

L et us celebrate this great and glorious feast of the Resurrection of the Lord, let us celebrate it with joy and devotion; the Lord is risen and has reawakened the whole earth. Adam sinned and died; Christ did not sin, but died. This is a new and surprising reality: the first one sinned and died, but this one did not sin and died. What does this mean? He who did not sin died, but it was in order to free the other, who had died because he sinned, from the chains of death. This also occurs with money. It often happens that if someone cannot pay a debt, he is put in prison; then another, who is not a debtor but has the money to pay the debt, frees him. So it happened in the case of Adam: Adam was a debtor, kept in prison by the devil but without money to pay. Christ was not a debtor to anyone and was not bound by chains, but he could pay. He came and gave his life for the one who was held captive by the devil, in order to free him.

John Chrysostom, *On the Resurrection*, 3-5

All of creation, the admirable work of God, delights in the Resurrection of Christ; but humanity, made "in the image and likeness of God" and to whom all creation was entrusted so that it might be faithfully and properly administered, delights in it all the more. Someone who receives good news or a special gift must absolutely recount it to someone else in order to share the great joy that he or she feels. In a similar way, we are called to recount the goodness of the gifts we have received through our words and deeds, so that everyone might participate in the final banquet in festive attire.

Christ was crucified the day before yesterday, but last night he rose; all of them were still slaves to sin the day before yesterday, but they rose with Christ: his body had died and his body rose, they were dead from sin and, freed from sin, they rose. The earth in this springtime produces roses, violets, and other flowers; the waters have provided us with a field more luscious than the earth. Do not be amazed that the waters give rise to flowers. It is not the earth that produces them by its nature; it produces them by God's command. In the beginning of things, the waters also produced animals endowed with movement. "May the waters produce living souls," he commanded, and the work that was ordered came forth, and that substance which did not have a single soul brought forth beings with souls. Likewise he said, "May the waters now bring forth not living reptiles, but spiritual gifts": the waters had produced dumb and mute fish before; now they produced intelligent and spiritual fish, which were fished by the Apostles. "Come after me, and I will make you fishers of men" (Mt 4:19): this is the fishing of which I spoke.

It is a new way of fishing: fishermen pull their catch out of the water, but we immerse sinners in the water of Baptism. That is how we fish. . . .

Do you see the grandeur of the gift? But now, my dear friend, preserve the grandeur of this gift. You cannot live in indifference. Inscribe the law well in your mind. This life is a battle: those who fight on the battlefield can defend themselves well from anything that might thwart victory.

IN THE OCTAVE OF EASTER

MONDAY

Theodore of Mopsuestia, *Catechetical Homily on Baptism (III)*, 5

After a sorrowful event that touches us closely, we all would love to wake up tomorrow as if it had just been a bad dream. Christ's Resurrection is that good awakening, the light that penetrates through the cracks in the window frames each morning, the dew that refreshes nature, and the divine reality that overcomes fear of death and becomes the last word.

At one time, before the coming of Christ, death had true power over us and was fully indestructible in virtue of a divine verdict. Its power over us was immense. But through his Death and Resurrection, Christ our Lord abrogated that law and destroyed the power of death. And by now the death of those who believe in Christ resembles a long sleep. As St. Paul says, "But now Christ has been raised from the dead, the firstfruits of those who have fallen asleep" (1 Cor 15:20). Since Christ our Lord has subdued the strength of death with his own Resurrection, we can say, "We who are baptized in Christ Jesus have been baptized in his Death"; in other words, we know that Christ our Lord has killed death.

Tuesday

Cyril of Jerusalem, *Catechetical Lectures XVIII, 6*

"For God all things are possible" (Mt 19:26). From this statement, and through a special "yes," the omnipotence of God became fully manifest to humanity. What nature is always telling us through the changing of the seasons and the planted seed that bears fruit, and what human imagination and genius show us through art, will finally become clear at the end of time. Doubting the Resurrection means doubting God: doubting the God for whom all things are possible.

A felled tree will blossom again; will not fallen man blossom again? What was sown and reaped sits in the barnyard; will not man, once cut off from this world, sit in the barnyard? The branches of vines and trees, when completely cut off, receive life and bear fruit if grafted on; will not man, for whom plants exist, resurrect after being buried? Comparatively speaking, which task is the greater: creating a statue that did not exist before, or remaking one that was broken, using the same form? Cannot God, who made us out of nothing, make those who lived and are now dead rise again? . . . Those things that were created for us come back to life once dead; will not we, for whom they live, rise again once dead?

Wednesday

Cyril and John of Jerusalem, *Mystagogical Catecheses II, 5*

In the exchange of Christ for humanity, we only have to gain: his all for our nothing—who would not call that a bargain? Yes, it's all strange and unimaginable, but who thinks they can know God's plans? Perhaps we do, who do not even really know who we truly are? Our task is to trust in him and to carry our cross, always looking to him.

O strange and paradoxical thing! We are not truly dead, nor truly buried, nor truly crucified and risen, but imitation by image brings true salvation. Christ was truly crucified and truly buried, and he is truly risen. So many graces are lavished upon us because we imitate him by participating in his suffering, and true salvation is earned. O boundless mercy! Christ even received nails in his hands and suffered; instead, salvation has been granted for me through participation, without suffering or agony.

Thursday

Dorotheus of Gaza, *Directions on the Spiritual Life*, XVI, 167

This is Dorotheus's explanation of some of St. Gregory's words, which are sung as a troparion for Easter. In the Byzantine Liturgy, a "troparion" is the main prayer repeated during the Liturgy of the Eucharist and at every Hour of the Divine Office. It is a sort of stanza that can be repeated either alone or as an element in a larger composition. We are called by St. Gregory and Dorotheus to joyfully give ourselves as an Easter offering in the manner of Christ, who rose for us.

Thus today is the Easter of the Lord, a day of glorious celebration, the day of the Resurrection of Christ, who crucified sin and died and rose for us. Let us then also present gifts to the Lord: victims and holocausts, but not of unreasoning animals, which Christ does not want. . . . But the Lamb of God was sacrificed for us, as the Apostle tells us: Christ, our Passover, was sacrificed for us, to take away the sins of the world [see, e.g., 1 Cor 5:7; Jn 1:29]. . . . For this reason, we too should present him with a gift that is pleasing to him. What gift, then, or what sacrifice should we present to Christ on the day of the resurrection that will be pleasing to him, since he does not want sacrifices of unreasoning animals? The same saint [St. Gregory] teaches us the answer, following his statement that "it is the day of resurrection" with these words: "let us present ourselves as an offering."

FRIDAY

Ephrem the Syrian, *Hymns*, 6-14

Jesus makes all things new. In him everything acquires a new light and a new life. Men and women are configured to Christ, and the shadows of sin are dispelled and dissipated by the light of the Lamb of God. What was once veiled or hidden is now visible and manifest to us: it is the Truth that makes us free and turns us into credible witnesses.

The Lord ate at Passover with his disciples. With the bread he broke, he abolished the unleavened bread. His bread that gives life to all gave life to the peoples; it replaced the unleavened bread that gave no life.

The Church has given us living bread in place of the unleavened bread that Egypt had given. Mary has given us the bread of life in place of the bread of weariness that Eve had given us. Abel was the lamb and offered up the lamb. Who ever heard of a lamb offering up a lamb?

The Lamb of God ate the lamb. Who ever heard of a lamb eating a lamb? The Lamb of Truth ate the Passover lamb. The symbol was eaten by the Truth.

All the symbols were waiting in the Holy of Holies for he who fulfills them all. The symbols saw the Lamb of Truth, opened the gates of the temple, and went to meet him. All the symbols entered into him and remained in him, and all of them spoke of him everywhere.

SATURDAY

John Chrysostom, *Homilies on the Gospel of Matthew*, 50, 2ff.

At the school run by his pastor—St. John Vianney, the Curé of Ars—a humble peasant from Ars had learned to stop in the church before beginning his work and after he completed it. One day, when his fellow laborer did not see him arrive, he knew where to find him. He entered the church and found him absorbed in prayer. He asked him why he was late, and the peasant simply responded, "I am looking at him, and he is looking at me," as if to say, "I am looking at him, Christ the Eucharist, and trying to understand myself in the light of his gaze."

And so we too touch the hem of his garment; indeed, if we wish, we can have all of Christ complete. His body is in fact before us now: not simply his garment, but his very body; and not just to touch it, but to eat of it and be filled by it. Let us therefore approach him with faith, each of us bringing his own weaknesses. If those who touched the hem of his garment drew such healing virtue from it, then those who receive Jesus Christ whole and complete can expect to draw even more. Nevertheless, approaching Christ with faith does not mean simply taking what he offers, but means touching him with a pure heart and a fervent disposition, knowing that we are drawing closer to Christ in person. What does it matter if you do not hear his voice? You contemplate him on the altar; or better yet, you also hear his voice, for he speaks to you through the Evangelists.

Believe with living faith that this is even now the same supper in which Christ took part with the Apostles. Indeed there is no difference between the Last Supper and the supper of the altar. Nor can it be said that this supper is celebrated by a man and the other by Christ, because Jesus himself performs them both. Well then, when you see the priest present this sacred food to you, do not think that it is the priest who gives it to you, but know that it is the hand of Christ outstretched toward you.

SECOND WEEK OF EASTER

DIVINE MERCY SUNDAY

John Chrysostom, *Homilies on the Gospel of Matthew*, 50, 2ff.

Just as Christ did not keep his divinity for himself, when he made himself man and offered himself as an innocent victim for the good of all, we too are called to do so for our brothers and sisters. But who are our brothers and sisters, who is our neighbor? Is it not enough to pray in the mornings and evenings and to go to Mass every Sunday? Is it not enough to obey the commandments and be good people? If it is enough, let's ask the homeless in our cities, the women exploited on the corners, the children forced to deal drugs, the lonely sick and elderly persons, and the unemployed fathers with a family to support . . .

Do you wish to honor Christ's body? Well then, do not tolerate his being unclothed; after having adorned him here in the church with silk fabrics, do not allow him to die of cold outside because of his nakedness. He who said, "This is my body," confirming by his words the action that he carried out, also said, "For I was hungry and you gave me no food" (Mt 25:42), and "what you did not do for one of these least ones, you did not do for me" (Mt 25:45). The Body of Christ on the altar needs no garments, but pure souls; but the one outside has need of great care. Let us therefore learn to think and act appropriately in accordance with such profound mysteries, and to honor Christ as he wishes to be honored. The most pleasing worship we can give to him, whom we desire to venerate, is what he himself wants and not what we think. Even Peter thought he was honoring Christ by preventing him from washing his feet, but that was not honor; rather, it was dishonor. Thus you too must honor him in the way that he himself has commanded, in other words, using your wealth to help the poor. God does not need gilded vases, but golden souls.

MONDAY

John Chrysostom, *Homilies on the Second Letter to Timothy*, 4, 4

Just as we find bread and wine on our own family table, so we also find them on the table of God's family—the altar—and on Jesus' table when he ate with the Apostles at the Last Supper. The Apostles immediately realized that it was not a meal like any other, and for this reason they preserved the memory in their hearts and continued its remembrance in the name of Jesus after he returned to the Father. To this very day, in every place on earth, priests repeat Jesus' actions at the Last Supper during the Mass.

The offering made is the same, whoever the offerer may be: whether Peter or Paul, it is the same offering that Christ gave to his disciples and that priests present to his followers today. This offering, which is made by priests today, is not in any way inferior to the offering Christ made at that time. This is because it is not the priest who consecrates it, but Christ himself who consecrated the first offering. Indeed, just as the words God spoke are the same ones that the priest says today, so the offering is the same; and our Baptism today is the same as Christ's Baptism. In other words, everything comes back in the context of faith. Thus, it is the Body of Christ that we give now, just as it was the Body of Christ that he gave to his disciples then; and those who think that what we now give is inferior in any way to what Christ gave demonstrate that they have not understood how it is still Christ who is present and acting today.

TUESDAY

Leo the Great, *Sermon 59*, 8

Loving one's enemy is truly difficult, but living as risen persons in Christ urges us to do even the impossible. We have to believe that it is possible today, that the wolf and lamb can graze together, that the poor and the wealthy can go arm in arm, and that the North and South of the world can mutually sustain one another. We have to believe that the impossible will happen, that death is defeated and life has won!

God's mercy toward us is even more surprising because of the fact that Christ died not for the just or the saints, but for the unjust and the sinners; and since he could not die because of his divine nature, he was born of human flesh and offered that humanity for us. Through the words of the prophet Hosea, God once taunted our death with the power of his own death by saying, "Where are your plagues, O death! / Where is your sting, O nether world!" (Hos 13:14). Indeed, by dying he was subjected to the laws of hell, but by rising he destroyed them and thereby shattered the perpetuity of death, altering it from eternal to temporal. Indeed, just as we all die in Adam, so we all rise in Christ.

Let us therefore do what the apostle Paul says, O dearly beloved: may "those who live . . . no longer live for themselves but for him who for their sake died and was raised" (2 Cor 5:15). And since the old order has passed and now everything has been made new, may no one remain stuck in the old way of life.

WEDNESDAY

Romanos the Melodist, *Hymn XI on the Resurrection*, 12

May the news of the Resurrection still resound today as it did two thousand years ago; may it resound with the same strength and courage of Mary; may it resound with awe and joy; may it resound and awaken the sleeping hearts of all men and women; may it resound and may all make haste to celebrate, both women and men, the young and the old, the sick and the healthy, the poor and the wealthy; may it resound in the world with tangible signs for every heart and every family, for all nations and all peoples.

May your tongue now issue these things, O woman, and may you explain them to the children of the Kingdom who are waiting for me, the Living Christ, to awaken. Run, O Mary, to gather my disciples in haste. You are a powerful trumpet sounding for me; may you play a song of peace for the fearful ears of my friends in hiding. Reawaken them all from their partial sleep, so that they will come to my meeting and light the candles. Go and tell them, "The spouse has awakened and has left the tomb without a trace upon his exit. May you now dispel all lethal sadness on your own, O Apostles, for he who has offered resurrection to the deceased has awakened."

Thursday

Augustine, *Sermon Guelpherbytanus 5*

The day of the Lord is solemn: it is Easter, alleluia! Celebrating Easter today means testifying in a loud voice that death will not have the upper hand, that what once seemed lost is now found, that the confusion is over, because Jesus died and rose so that we might live. He urges us this day not to live for ourselves, but to "bear one another's burdens" (Gal 6:2).

The day of the Lord's Passion, therefore, the day on which he was crucified, already followed the true Passover night, and thus it came to a close and ended with the Parasceve—which the Jews also simply call supper—on the commencement of the night that begins the observance of the Sabbath. Thus the day of the Sabbath, which begins on that night, ends on evening of the following night, which is the beginning of the Lord's Day: the Lord thereby sanctified this day through the glory of his Resurrection. We now celebrate this remembrance of the solemnity of that night up through the beginning of the day that belongs to the Lord.

We pass that night in vigil, for it was then that the Lord rose and united within his flesh that life of which we just spoke, where there is neither death nor sleep; and it was then that he was resurrected from the dead so he would no longer die and so death would no longer have any sway over him.

Indeed, since the body was not found in the tomb when it was sought in the early morning by those who loved him, and the angels told them he had already risen, it is clear that he rose during that night which drew to a close at dawn. Thus by our vigil let us sing ever more hymns of praise to him who is risen, so that through our lives we may reign with him forever.

But if by chance his body has still been in the tomb and has not yet risen precisely during these hours in which we are keeping vigil, we would not be incoherent by keeping this vigil: for he slept so that we might wake, and he died so that we might live.

Friday

Cyril of Jerusalem, *Catechetical Lectures* XX, 2-8

All people must confide only in Jesus Christ for salvation. Foolish are they who become attached to material goods, false idols, passing ideologies, unbridled science, their own empty selfishness, the power of evil, and false prophets. Not only have we died with Christ, but we will rise with him (see, e.g., Rom 6:5; 1 Cor 6:14): through his real suffering, he has brought us into his divine and mysterious plan for eternal salvation.

O new and inconceivable fact! We did not truly die, nor were we truly buried, nor did we truly rise after being crucified. We have only imitated these events symbolically, but salvation is instead a reality! Christ was truly crucified, truly buried, and truly rose again. And he granted us all of this by his grace, so that we might truly obtain salvation by symbolically participating in his suffering. O overflowing goodness! Christ accepted the nails in his uncontaminated hands and feet, and suffered because of them; instead, salvation has been granted for me without my suffering and labor, through symbolic participation in his suffering. . . . Precisely in order to teach us that what Christ underwent for us and for our salvation was true and not just apparent suffering, and that we participate in his suffering, Paul proclaimed with utter clarity: "For if we have grown into union with him through a death like his, we shall also be united with him in the resurrection" (Rom 6:5). . . . Death was a reality for Christ: his soul was truly separated from his body and his tomb was real; his sacred body was wrapped in the clean shroud and authentically underwent everything. For us, it is instead a question of a symbol of death and suffering; the salvation obtained, however, is not a symbol but a reality.

SATURDAY

Leo the Great, *Sermon 71* (58)

Yes, the Resurrection of Jesus is a mysterious event, but one that was made manifest right from the first moment to the disciples and to the world through the descent of the Holy Spirit on the nascent Church. The tomb is empty, Christ is truly risen! The Resurrection does not imply abandonment; but rather Christ was present with his followers as a teacher, so that they might see, believe, and witness. Today he is present among us, so that we might be his courageous witnesses.

The Resurrection of the Savior did not therefore keep his soul in hell or his body in the tomb for long; life returned so quickly to his incorrupt flesh that he seemed to have been more asleep than deceased. His divinity, which actually had not abandoned the two components of the human nature he assumed, reunited by divine power what that power had separated. Many pieces of evidence followed, which were destined to ground the authority of the faith that would be preached throughout the world: the stone that was rolled away, the empty tomb, the folded sheet, and the angels who recounted what happened. These things give solid support to the truth of the Resurrection of the Lord. No less important are the appearances of the Lord to the women and multiple times to the Apostles: not only did he briefly encounter them, but he even stayed with them at length, ate in their company, and allowed himself to be examined closely and touched with curiosity by those who doubted. Indeed, he entered the room with locked doors where his disciples were gathered, gave them the Holy Spirit by breathing upon them, shed light upon their intellects, opened the secrets of the Scriptures to them, and even showed them the wound in his side, the holes of the nails, and all of the signs of his recent Passion. All of this was done to show them that the properties of his divine nature and those of his human nature were distinct in him, and so that they might learn that the Word is not identical to the flesh, but rather that the Son of God is at the same time both Word and flesh.

THIRD WEEK
OF EASTER

SUNDAY

Leo the Great, *Sermon 71* (58)

The current liturgical periods are an occasion to renew our adherence to the Gospel, but they are not fleeting and limited, just as our participation cannot be merely formal or confined to these few days of the year. Christians are not sentimentalists, and devotion cannot be reduced to ritualism. Baptism entails recognizing the gifts received and a commitment to witnessing every day of our lives.

May the People of God thus recognize that they are a new creature in Christ, and may they be sure to understand who it is that has adopted them and from whom they have received adoption. May that which has been renewed not return to its past instability, and may he who has put his hands to the plow not abandon his work (see Lk 9:62); instead, may he look carefully at what he has sown, and not set his gaze on what he has abandoned. May no one fall back into the vices out of which he has risen; but even if he should again give in to the weaknesses of the flesh, may he desire without delay to be washed and healed. This is the way of salvation, this is the way to imitate the Resurrection whose origin is in

Christ; and given that it will be impossible to avoid falling or tripping on the icy road of life, may the steps of the travelers leave the unstable ground for solid ground, for it is written that "those whose steps are guided by the LORD; / whose way God approves, / may stumble, but they will never fall, / for the LORD holds their hand" (Ps 37:23).

This meditation, dearly beloved, is not just fitting for the feast of Easter alone, but we should take it to heart in order to sanctify our entire lives. These spiritual exercises should tend to transform practices—whose brief experience has been a source of joy for faithful souls—into habits, preserve their purity, and shatter with a ready penance the guilt of any sin that might catch us off-guard. Healing old wounds is a long and difficult process: therefore the more recent the wounds are, the more quickly may we apply the remedy, so that by always rising completely after each fall, we might merit through Jesus Christ our Lord the attainment of that incorruptible resurrection of the body, called to glorification.

MONDAY

Athanasius, *Easter Letter I*, 292-294

He paid Adam's debt to the Eternal Father for us, and with the blood he shed for our salvation he wiped out the punishment for that Original Sin. This is the true Easter, in which the true Lamb was killed, who consecrated the homes of the faithful with his blood. This is the night in which you freed the children of Israel, our fathers, from slavery in Egypt, and brought them unharmed across the Red Sea. This is the night in which you defeated the darkness of sin with the splendor of the pillar of fire. This is the night that saves believers in Christ all over the earth from the darkness of sin and worldly corruption, consecrates them to the love of the Father, and unites them in the Communion of Saints. (See Exultet, Easter Vigil.)

By now the time of symbolic figures has passed, and we no longer act in their manner; but rather we are turned toward the Lord, who is spirit, and where there is spirit there is freedom, which the priestly trumpeters re-echo in our ears. Indeed, we no longer sacrifice a material lamb, but the true Lamb, who was condemned to the slaughter like a sheep, who remained silent as a lamb before the slaughterer, and who purified us with his Precious Blood, which speaks greater volumes than that of Abel.

Now that the enemy and tyrant of the world has been defeated, we participate no longer in a temporal feast, but in an eternal and heavenly one; and we do not simply portray this in a figurative manner, but we do so truly. In the past, the feast was celebrated by eating the meat of an unreasoning lamb and marking the doors with its blood to keep the destroyer away. Now, instead, when we eat the Word of the Father and tinge the lips of our hearts with the blood of the New Testament, we recognize the grace of the Savior, who tells us, "I have given you the power 'to tread upon serpents' and scorpions and upon the full force of the enemy" (Lk 10:19). Death will no longer reign, and life will succeed death, for the Lord says, "I am . . . the life" (Jn 14:6). Everything now abounds with gladness and exults, just as it is written: "The LORD is king; let the earth rejoice" (Ps 97:1). Death reigned when we sat weeping on the banks of the rivers of Babylonia and were grieved by the bitterness of slavery. Now that death and the reign of the enemy have been destroyed, all things are filled with joyful gladness.

TUESDAY

Peter Chrysologus, *Sermon 74*

We can only imagine having experienced wonder and awe, fear and trepidation, if we had found ourselves before the empty tomb on Easter day. Christ is not there, he's no longer in that spot, he cannot be sought in that place of rest, but rather among those who live on in the Father's splendor. Blessed is he who believes without having seen or touched; blessed are we when we say our daily "yes" to the Author of life, even when everything around us seems dark and gloomy.

The earth trembled not because the angel of the Lord descended from heaven, but because the Lord ascended out of hell. And thus a great earthquake shook the ground.

Chaos erupted, the abysses of the earth were torn, the earth shook, the mountain masses trembled, the foundations of the universe were violently jolted, Tartarus was torn to pieces, and hell shifted: death, which was directed toward the guilty, met with the judge, and controlled by the servants it turned against the Lord, and raging against man it hurled itself at God. Rightly, then, the laws of hell vanished, its rights were taken away, and the power of death was stripped. . . . Finally, the bodies were given back, man was rehabilitated, life was restored, and all things are now made of forgiveness, because the sentence was immediately transferred onto the Author of life. . . .

With the defeat of death and the Risen Christ, Divine Revelation was restored to mortals; and to woman, for whom the advice of the devil had been fatal, the meeting with the angel became vital.

Indeed, the angel of the Lord descended from heaven and overturned the stone. It did not say "rolled away," but "overturned": once moved into place, it was proof of his death; once moved away, it confirmed the occurrence of the Resurrection. Blessed the stone that was graced to conceal and reveal Christ; blessed is he who opens his heart no less than the tomb; blessed is he who puts his faith in the Resurrection and in the resurrection of faith that testifies that the divine body is risen. The order of things changes with this event: here the tomb devours death and not the dead, and the dwelling place of death becomes the dwelling place of life. It is a new way for both: it conceives the dead and gives birth to the living.

Wednesday

Romanos the Melodist, *Hymn XLI*, 13, 18-20

A hymn is a poem: an elegant poem, as in the following selection. But what hymn and what words can truly give praise to the magnificence of God? What hymn could ever fully equal the voice that proclaims that Christ is risen? There are no words, but only stuttering and timid allusions, which are only human words. And yet God has made use of men and women, of their intelligence and their imaginations, to tell his "Good News." How amazing!

Christ the King had an army guarding him. Outside the tomb were the soldiers; inside was the battle of Christ against Death, where the former took power and the latter fell from it, where the former took over the slaves of hell, and the latter cried out to its subjects, "Let us shout: 'The Lord is risen!'" . . .

Now the night has passed—yes, it has truly passed—and what you said not long ago is true, my friend: he who was dead not long before is now luminous. It is he who overturned the stone from within, he who frightened us with his words, for he is terrifying. He brings the light, radiates the light, and is light. Without a doubt he is a son of light and a servant of light, just as the words cried out by the women attest: "The Lord is risen!"

Here is their grave and our recompense; the shame of the impious, and our title of glory; a wound for them, and life for us: it is that the Lord is truly risen. The tomb guards could have been given money to keep quiet, yes, but the stones shout it even louder: "A stone on the mountain removed without the aid of human hands, lifted away from the tomb like a child from his mother's breast, the Lord is risen!"

You, Lord, came from the womb without seed, leaving the Virgin with the signs of virginity, just as you destroyed the reign of the tomb today through the tomb. Leaving Joseph's linen in the tomb, you took back the linen of him who had generated Joseph: Adam came to follow you; Eve walked in your footsteps. Eve is the servant of Mary; the whole earth adores you, singing the victory hymn: "The Lord is risen!"

Thursday

Leo the Great, *Sermon 73*, 2-4

"Jesus reveals to us the meaning of the Scriptures as he did for his disciples on the road to Emmaus," so that every day might be new and every life might be full, but often our eyes are closed and our ears do not listen to the voice of the Shepherd. So it is that we fall to the mercy of vices, desperation, and sin, and we forget that we are heirs. Receiving the sacraments is therefore the best medicine to defeat blindness and deafness, and to feel our hearts aflame once more in his presence.

Dearly beloved, these days spanning the Resurrection of the Lord and his Ascension are not to be passed in idleness; instead, great mysteries have been confirmed and great truths have been revealed. It was during these days that the fear of a dreaded death was abolished and immortality was proclaimed not only for the soul, but also for the body. It was during these days that the Holy Spirit infused all the apostles through the breath of the Lord, and that the holy Apostle Peter—in a position of preference over the others—found himself entrusted with caring for the Lord's flock after receiving the keys to the Kingdom. It was during these days that the Lord walked alongside the two traveling disciples and, in order to clear away all doubt, challenged their slowness of belief as they trembled in fear. The hearts that he enlightened felt the flame of faith burn within them, and those who were lukewarm became fervent when the Lord opened the Scriptures to them. The faces of those sitting at table lit up at the moment of the breaking of the bread, and their eyes opened to see the glory of their nature made manifest.

FRIDAY

Leo the Great, *Sermon 74*, 1-3, 5

Being in the presence of the Father and returning to him after the earthly pilgrimage belonged to the experience of Christ. Instead, we who have not merited such grace are brought into heaven, where hope becomes fulfilled, charity becomes the essence of all, and faith becomes all-encompassing. We were once blind, but when we ascend with Christ we will need neither sunlight nor artificial light.

On the occasion of the feast of Easter, the Resurrection of the Lord is the cause for our joy; today, his Ascension into heaven gives us new reason for joy. We fittingly commemorate and venerate this day in which the humility of our nature was raised, in Christ, above all the angelic orders and the sublimity of all the powers to finally share the throne of God the Father. It is upon this arrangement of the divine works that we are established and edified; in truth, the grace of God becomes more marvelous when it keeps faith from doubting, hope from wavering, and charity from waning now that he who deserved the respect of men by his physical presence has disappeared from their sight. This, in effect, is the strength of great spirits and the characteristic light of eminently faithful souls: it consists in unshakably believing what the eyes of the body do not see and setting their desire where sight cannot reach.

SATURDAY

Athanasius, *Easter Letter I*, 292-294

Living as Risen People means putting on the garments of a new life, though not just in appearance or custom, but in the certainty that Christ has risen. It is not a virtual experience, nor is it a story to tell in words alone; it is life itself, which tells of God's wonders through the struggle against sins both great and small, and through humble and constant service to the weakest of our brothers and sisters.

Nor is it in Judea alone that the Lord is renowned; but his fame has spread throughout the entire world, and the whole earth is filled with knowledge of the Lord. It is also clear, my dearly beloved, that we who participate in such a feast should not wear dirty garments, but should rather put on the cleanest of clothing on this feast day of our Lord Jesus, in order to truly celebrate the feast with him. And we will most certainly be dressed in this way when we love virtue and flee from vice, when we observe chastity and avoid lust, when we prefer justice to injustice, when we strengthen our spirit by being content with what is strictly necessary, when we do not forget the poor but rather open our doors to all, and when we try to humble our spirit and detest pride.

Even Israel once zealously carried out this rite, as if figuratively, and participated in the feast; but at the time, these things were like representations and silhouettes. Instead we, my dearly beloved, having no more figures and having set aside all shadow, cannot consider this feast representative or approach the Passover altar as they do in the earthly Jerusalem according to the indefinite vigil of the Jews, so that we will not appear to be working outside of time with the passing of time; rather, following the example of the apostles, we must leave behind those figures and sing the new song.

FOURTH WEEK OF EASTER

SUNDAY

Pseudo-Macarius, *Spiritual Homilies*, 12, 4-5

"I want to be like you" is the most beautiful phrase that a parent, teacher, or educator can hear from a young person: not "I want to do," but rather "I want to be"! So we, too, like all the apostles and saints who have preceded us and walk with us, are called to be like Jesus, to set our feet in his footsteps even when the road is paved with thorns.

I f God acted as he did on this earth, then it is up to us to imitate him; if the apostles and the prophets did not fall short, then we too must follow them on the same road if we wish to build on the foundations laid by the Lord and the Apostles. . . . If, on the other hand, you aspire to human glory and desire to receive honor and be respected, and you are looking for a life of comfort, it means that you have already lost the path you should be following. Indeed, it is necessary for you to suffer and be crucified together with him who was crucified, in order to be glorified together with him who was glorified. In essence, without the cost of suffering and persevering along a bitter, narrow, and arduous path, it is impossible to enter the city of the saints and reign together with the King through all eternity.

Monday

Clement of Rome, *Second Letter to the Corinthians*, 8-9

Jesus came to heal the sick and care for our human weakness. So long as we still have the chance to be cared for, may we entrust ourselves to God, our doctor, without neglecting to give him his honorarium. Is it even possible to completely repay our debt? That can only happen if we truly repent in the depths of our heart, and learn how to stake our lives on unconditional love.

Let us do penance so long as we are still on this earth, dear brothers, for we are like clay in the hands of the potter. So long as the pot breaks or becomes misshapen while the potter is still molding it, he can set his hand to it once more; but otherwise, if he has already put it in the oven, there is no longer anything he can do about it. We too, dear brothers, can repent with all our heart of our sins committed in the flesh so long as we remain on this earth, thereby obtaining salvation from the Lord while we are still in time; once we have left this world, however, we will no longer be able to do penance and confess our sins. Thus, dear brothers, we will gain eternal life only if we comply with the will of the Father, keeping our bodies pure and fulfilling the commandments of the Lord. . . . Therefore let us love one another, so that we might all reach the Kingdom of God.

Tuesday

Basil the Great, *Homily for Judith the Martyr*, 3-4

With our thoughts turned to God and our hearts turned to the needs of our brothers and sisters, we can unceasingly pray with a prayer not limited to words alone, but rather united to God in all of our actions in life, so that our very lives may become a constant and continuous prayer. Invocations are short, simple, and intense prayers that can be repeated mentally, but every act of love for our neighbor can also be a form of praising God.

A prayer is a request for a good directed to God by a believer. We do not consider this request limited to words. Indeed, we do not believe that God needs words to remember, for he knows what we need even if we do not pray for it. But what do we mean by this? That our prayer should not consist of just syllables, but should rather find its strength in the choices of the soul, and in the practice of the virtues throughout our life. . . . When sitting at table, pray; when taking your bread, thank him who grants it to you. . . . May you never cease remembering your benefactor. If you put on a garment, thank him who gave it to you; if you throw a cloak around your shoulders, may you grow in love for God who provides for us in summer and winter. . . . Has the day ended? Thank him who gives us the sun for daytime work and who grants us fire to light up the night and serve the other needs of life. May the night thus bring you other reasons to pray. When you lift your eyes to heaven and stare at the beauty of the stars, pray to the Lord of all these visible things and adore God, the sublime maker of the universe, who created all things with wisdom.

WEDNESDAY

Ephrem the Syrian, *The Second Coming of Our Lord*, 24-25

Jesus is the healer of souls and bodies, hope for the hopeless, safe landing for those who are battered by the storm, help for those who are helpless, the way of life who calls everyone to repentance and does not send away anyone who converts. We too find refuge in him, because all sinners who turn to him obtain salvation for their souls.

Beware; let no one say, "I have not sinned." He who says so is blind and nearsighted; he fools himself and does not see how Satan deceives him in his words and works, through his hearing, touching, and thinking. Who can take glory in having an immaculate heart and purity in all the senses? No one is without sin, no one is without uncleanliness, no one among all men has ever been without error, except for he alone who, though rich, became poor for our sake. Only he who takes away the sins of the world is without sin, he who desires the sanctity of all men and does not desire the death of a sinner: he who is a friend to men, the most Meek and Merciful One, the Good Lover of souls, the Omnipotent, the Savior of all men, the Father of the wise, the Judge of widows, and the God of penitents.

Thursday

Lactantius, *Epitome of the Divine Institutes*, 67

"The human heart is heavy and hardened. God must give man a new heart. Conversion is first of all a work of the grace of God who makes our hearts return to him: 'Restore us to thyself, O LORD, that we may be restored!' (Lam 5:21). God gives us the strength to begin anew. It is in discovering the greatness of God's love that our heart is shaken by the horror and weight of sin and begins to fear offending God by sin and being separated from him. The human heart is converted by looking upon him whom our sins have pierced" (*Catechism of the Catholic Church*, 2nd. ed., no. 1432 [Washington, DC: Libreria Editrice Vaticana–United States Conference of Catholic Bishops, 2000]).

Our fragile nature does not allow anyone to be without blemish. So it is that our best remedy is to take refuge in repentance, which holds an important place among the virtues since it is self-improvement: thus, if we fall either in word or in deed, we immediately mend our ways, confess that we have sinned, and ask for forgiveness from God, who in his mercy does not deny it unless we persist in our error. The help of penance is great; its consolation is abundant. It is healing from the wounds of sin; it is hope, the harbor of salvation. He who denies it takes away that which gives life to one's life, because no one can be so upright that penitence is not at times necessary. But even if we have not sinned, we must nonetheless open our souls to God and implore him all the same because of our failings, thanking him even in the midst of adversity. Let us always give God our obedience; indeed, humility is pleasing and dear to him. Since he much more gladly welcomes a converted sinner than a prideful righteous man, how much more will he welcome a just man who confesses his wrongdoings, lifting him high in the Kingdom of Heaven in accordance with the measure of his humility!

FRIDAY

Rabbula of Edessa, *Liturgical Hymns*, 1-3

The salvation of a sinful person is only in God. His initiative to help us must be met with our decision to reconcile ourselves with him and with others. He awaits us like the merciful father in the Gospel parable: not forcing or pushing us, but patiently waiting. He is ready to celebrate our return, but it's up to us to recognize the little that we are, to stand up, and to walk back toward our true home.

You who are rich with mercy and grace, you who wash all sinners of their guilt, cleanse me with your purifying hyssop and have mercy on me! In your mercy, be gentle with me as you once were with the tax collector and the woman who sinned! Christ, you who forgive the trespasses of sinners and welcome all penitents, O Redeemer of the human race, redeem me likewise in your mercy! Even a righteous man will be saved only through toil and with difficulty: what then should I, a sinner, do? I did not bear the weight of the day and the blazing heat of the sun, but I am one of those who only began working at the eleventh hour. Save me and have mercy on me! My sins have leveled me to the ground; they have thrown me down from the heights where I stood. I have thrown myself into perdition as though into a pit. Who could now give me back my radiant beauty if not you, O most wise Creator, who in the beginning created me in your image and likeness? I voluntarily made myself a slave to sin: in your mercy free me, O Lord, and have mercy on me!

SATURDAY

Leo the Great, *Sermon 6*

Doing good to others is doing good to ourselves! Christ will one day ask us whether we have multiplied the gifts entrusted to us for the good of our brothers and sisters, and what we have done to support those who are impoverished and abandoned. What will we say? That this is just the way the world works, and we could not do anything? If this were our response, what meaning would the commandment of love have had for us? If we have not done everything possible for the good of others, then we have not done so for ourselves.

It is certain that each of us does good to his soul whenever he mercifully tends to the needs of others. Therefore, O dearly beloved, our beneficence must be ready and quick if we believe that each of us gives to himself whatever he bestows upon those in need. He who feeds Christ in the poor man stores his treasure in heaven. In this you recognize the gentleness and the economy of divine mercy: he wanted you to have in abundance so that, through you, your neighbor would not remain in need, and through the service of this good work you free the poor man from his needs and yourself from the multitude of your sins. O admirable Providence and goodness of the Creator, who willed that help for two people be found in a single act! Next Sunday, then, will be the collection. Appealing to your holiness, I urge and counsel you all to remember the poor and yourselves, and within the limits of your possibilities, to see Christ in those in need, Christ who so urgently entrusted us with the poor as to affirm that we clothe, welcome, and feed him in them.

FIFTH WEEK OF EASTER

SUNDAY

Athenagoras, *On the Resurrection of the Dead*, 13

Lent has not driven us toward disdain for the body as such, because we must recognize it as a precious gift from God. We need to overcome morbid attachment to it or the debasement of its dignity in order to prepare ourselves for the Resurrection and for when our mortal body will shine with God's fullness.

Considering our nature, we certainly love this present life, despite how defective and corruptible it is, because it suits our present reality; however, we firmly hope to live forever in an incorruptible state. And this hope is not founded on an empty invention of the human imagination, feeding us with vain hopes, because we instead believe in the most infallible Guarantor, in the plan of he who created us, a plan in which man is composed of a body and an immortal soul endowed with reason and an inherent law suited to a rational life and an intelligent existence so that man might save and protect what was granted him. We are convinced that he would not have made such a being, endowing him with all the means for eternal existence, if he had not desired for him to remain in eternity.

Monday

Theophilus of Antioch, *To Autolycus*, 1, 13

Everything tells of the greatness of God, and the wonders of creation praise his magnificence. May all human beings, the Creator's favored creature, rediscover themselves as "children" who have been loved and chosen, blessed and offered, who have risen in Christ, and who will one day be joyful inhabitants with the angels and saints in heaven. Let's realize what we have been created for and live in the hope of the good things God has prepared for us.

I f you wish to see a more marvelous sight demonstrating the Resurrection, do not look only to the earth, but also to the sky: consider the resurrection of the moon occurring month by month, how it wanes, disappears, and resurrects. And listen further, O man, for the resurrection that occurs in you though you do not know it. Perhaps you have fallen sick on occasion, and have lost your flesh, your strength, and your beauty; but once you received mercy and healing from God, you regained your weight, your good shape, and your strength. Just as you did not know where your flesh went as it atrophied, so you do not know where it comes from and what it is formed from. But perhaps you say, "From food and drink, which are transformed into flesh." Excellent! But this too is the work of God, who made it so, and of none other.

TUESDAY

John Damascene, *An Exposition of the Orthodox Faith*, 4, 27

God the Father is good and never breaks his promises. Faith helps us believe in his mercy and look to earthly life as an opportunity to fulfill his design of love for us. Let's not be stopped by our human fears; instead, may we faithfully throw ourselves into the arms of the Father with the simplicity of a child.

We also believe in the resurrection of the dead. It will certainly happen: the resurrection of the dead will occur. When we say "resurrection," we mean the resurrection of the body. Resurrection is when those who have fallen rise again for the second time; but how will souls, which are immortal, resurrect? If death is defined as the separation of the soul from the body, the resurrection is evidently a new union of the soul with the body, a renewed emergence of the fallen and decomposed being. Therefore the body, corrupt and decomposed, will also arise incorrupt. He who made it in the beginning from the dust of the earth certainly does not lack the power to make it rise again—in accordance with the judgment of the Creator—after it has decomposed and returned to the dust from which it was formed.

WEDNESDAY

Gregory of Nyssa, *Love for the Poor*, 1

The following words seem written in our time, yet they come from many centuries ago. The poor are with us, among us, knocking at our door or sitting and sleeping on our doorstep. And what do we do? What are we prepared to lose for those who suffer? Do we trust Jesus? Are we ready to be judged by the world? Are we able to make decisions that go against the mainstream? Love as he loves: are we ready to give our lives?

The number of naked and homeless people that our time has brought us is great. . . . There is no shortage of immigrants and refugees, and everywhere one turns there are hands outstretched in supplication. For them, home is the sky and the open air; porticos, intersections, and isolated corners in public squares are their shelter. . . . Their clothes are ragged; their victuals are the good will of the merciful; their food is what is given them by chance; their drink is from the springs with the animals; their cup is the hollow of their hands; their closet is their clothing, provided it is not too ragged and covers what is put there; their table is their knees held together; their bed is the ground. . . . Provide for them, O you who fast. Be generous in the face of your brothers' misfortunes. . . . What you give is certainly not a loss. Do not fear: the fruit of almsgiving blossoms flourishingly. Sow your gifts and you will fill your house with beautiful sheaves.

THURSDAY

Cyril of Jerusalem, *Catechetical Lectures XVIII*, 1

The prize is here and it's visible! It is seen in the eyes of God and in the perspective of Christian hope. We have to work to reach it, sweetly toiling, constantly training, keeping it always before us as the objective, dream, and desire. If the prize is resurrection, and it is proclaimed by him who is Witness par excellence, then it's truly worth it to do good and to put all of our energy into the race.

The root of every good work is the hope of resurrection. Indeed, expectation of recompense sustains the soul in doing good deeds. Every good worker is prepared to put himself through the toil if he sees a profit in the toil itself. The soul lapses with the body for those who work without pay. The soldier who expects a combat medal is prepared for war. No one fighting for a king who lacks good judgment, who does not award recognition for the soldiers' toil, is ready to confront death for him. Thus, every soul that believes in the resurrection [of the body] also rightly takes good care of itself; instead, the soul that does not believe in the resurrection is consigned to ruin. He who believes that the body awaits the resurrection takes care how he dresses and does not contaminate his body through fornication.

FRIDAY

Gregory of Nazianzus, *On the Love for the Poor*, 8-9

As Christians we ground our roots in love, and in love of neighbor! This energy is so powerful that it helps us encounter joy and happiness even along the way to Calvary, the way of the Passion, and the way of the Cross. Love is not that sentiment that suddenly erupts, exploding and rapidly dissipating, but rather a free, conscious, and painstaking decision that fills us with calmness and gives meaning to everything that we do, even in the midst of tears.

We must take care of our neighbor's body no less than each of us takes care of his own, whether it is healthy or consumed by sickness. . . . Some people invite sympathy simply by their poverty; but perhaps time, work, a friend, a relative, or a good opportunity can change their situation. Others are no less pitiable, but rather much more so, insofar as they have no possibility of working and helping themselves and therefore lack the necessary things for life; for them, the fear of powerlessness is always greater than the hope of being well, so hope itself does little to help them, though it is the only medicine for the unfortunate. In addition to poverty, there is a second evil: sickness. It is the most detestable and oppressive of evils, and is the first thing invoked by many in their curses. The third evil is this: not being able to be visited or even looked upon, but being avoided, being the cause of nausea and even horror; for them, this is worse than the sickness itself. It is the impression of being hated because of their misfortune. I cannot speak of these people without tears of suffering, and I am deeply moved just thinking of them: may you experience these same feelings, and join your tears to mine.

SATURDAY

John Chrysostom, *Homilies on the Gospel of Matthew*, 50, 2ff.

Encountering Christ changes us both inside and out! Encountering him in the Sunday Eucharist or even every day is a "school of life" that leaves us transformed and requires intelligence of the heart and constancy of action on the path of goodness. There can be no hesitation or excuses, because "no one who sets a hand to the plow and looks to what was left behind is fit for the kingdom of God" (Lk 9:62). We cannot waste any time or put off being imitators of Christ and witnesses to his love for all.

Christ has allowed us to satiate ourselves with his flesh, he has offered himself as a sacrifice. What excuse do we have if we continue to sin while nourished in this way, if we live like wolves while sustained by the Lamb, if we do not cease being greedy as lions while strengthened by such food? This sacrament demands not only that we be constantly free of any violence and theft, but also that we be clean of even the smallest animosity. Indeed, this Sacrament is a sacrament of peace and does not permit having attachment to wealth. Jesus did not save himself for us: what justification can we call upon, therefore, to preserve our earthly goods while neglecting our soul, for which Christ did not save his life? God had instituted several annual feasts for the Jews in remembrance of his gifts; but for you, now, that remembrance exists every day through these sacred mysteries. Therefore, do not be ashamed of the Cross. These are our sacred truths, these are our mysteries; we adorn ourselves with this gift, we deck ourselves with it and boast of it. When I say that God has spread open the skies, unfurled the earth and the seas, and sent prophets and angels, I am saying nothing remotely comparable to this sacrament. The summit of all goods is in the fact that God did not preserve his own Son in order to save his servants who were hostile against him.

Sixth Week of Easter and the Ascension of the Lord

Sunday

Theophilus of Alexandria, *Easter Letter* (*AD 401*), 2

The Easter journey can be experienced as the preparation for a long-desired trip: we need to pick out the right clothes, check our state of health, get to know the places through maps or pictures, and still dream big. Our spiritual journey should also be similarly prepared: we need to abandon our garments of sin, recognize that we have been blessed, ponder over the Passion and the Resurrection, and hope in what we do not yet see.

Well then, imitating those table companions who celebrated the feast of the Passion of the Lord in like manner, let us sing together with St. David: "I shall praise the LORD all my life, / sing praise to my God while I live" (Ps 146:2). Let us also make haste toward the city of angels; it is free, it has no stain of sin defiling it, and within it there is no discord, no ruin, and no possibility of being banished from one place to another. Let us crush any sensual pleasures underfoot, halt the waves of lust that all too often rise up against us, and blend ourselves in with the heavenly choruses. Thus, if we are already there with our thoughts, then we are already there; and if our gaze is directed toward those most sacred places, then we can be now what we will one day become. The Jews became unworthy of this beatitude because they abandoned the treasures of the Sacred Scripture and passively followed the feeble thinking of their teachers, and this is what they are still heard saying today. Their heart is still in error so long as they refuse to say to Christ, who has come, "Blessed is he / who comes in the name of the LORD" (Ps 118:26), and all the more so because his miracles, which are more evident than any affirmation, constitute the proof of his divinity.

MONDAY

Leo the Great, *Sermon 16*

Easter urges us to look to Christ, to lift up our hearts on high without ever forgetting our brothers and sisters in need. Our conscience might be seemingly cleared by giving some economic contributions to the missions, giving an extra piece of change while waiting at a traffic light, or feeling sad when we see some terrible news on television. We can start here, but the goal is total involvement and time spent out of love.

The sublime grace of God, O dearly beloved, is working every day in Christian hearts, shifting our every desire from earthly goods to heavenly ones. But even our present life moves by a gift of the Creator and is sustained by his Providence: indeed, he who bestows temporal goods on us and promises eternal goods is one and the same. . . . The fullness of religiosity and justice demand that we too help others with the gifts that our heavenly Father has mercifully bestowed on us. Indeed, there are many who have nothing: neither fields nor vines nor olive trees; we must provide for their needs with the abundance that God has granted us, so that they may bless God together with us for the fertility of the earth and be glad that these goods were bestowed upon their owners, who share them with the poor and the strangers. Happy the granary—and worthy to have its fruits multiplied in him—that serves to satisfy the hunger of the weak and the needy, that serves to relieve the needs of strangers, and that alleviates the needs of the sick.

TUESDAY

Chromatius of Aquileia, *Sermon 15*, 1

"Look to God that you may be radiant" (Ps 34:6), says the psalmist; look to Jesus and be irradiated by his immense goodness and humility. He became like us so we could become like him! During a time that makes arrogance, personal glory, success, and image the most fundamental reasons for living, Christ, who makes himself a servant, vexes, disrupts, and often disturbs Christians themselves just as he "irritated" the disciples by washing their feet. Which model do we wish to follow?

There are certainly many examples of humility that our Lord and Savior offered us after having taken flesh through a virgin. But the greatest example of all is the one presented in the Scripture, when he deigned to wash the feet of his disciples. . . . This humility of the Lord is wonderful and incomparable. He, the Lord of eternal majesty, whom the angels serve in heaven, washed the feet of his servants and serves men on earth. He humbled himself on the earth so that you would not seek to exalt yourself in anything. He washed the feet of his disciples so that you would not scorn washing those of your fellow servants. You cannot exalt yourself for reason of wealth, birth, or honor, because it was the Lord of honor and power who deigned to carry this act all the way through. He showed us an example of humility that we must follow and imitate. Moreover, this gesture conceals a great mystery regarding our salvation.

WEDNESDAY

Leo the Great, *Sermon 71* (58)

Those who have encountered Jesus Christ and his Church can fully welcome the gospel message or choose to travel other roads. It is in freedom that we are saved and in freedom itself that we are loved. If we fall in love during this encounter, we will become new creatures, happy and excited to have abandoned our old ways and to live the present moment with the certainty of future goods.

For every man, in reality, passing through a conversion of any kind, from one state to another, signifies the end of one thing and the beginning of another: no longer being what he once was, and being what he was not before.

It is important to know, however, to whom we die and for whom we live, since there is a dying that makes us live and a living that makes us die. Now, it is only in the fleeting world that we seek both one and the other, such that the difference in our eternal compensation will depend on the quality of our actions. Thus, we die to the devil and we live for God; we die to injustice and rise for justice; the old condition vanishes and the new one arises; and since, according to the word of Truth, no one can serve two masters, let us take as our master not him who undermines those who are standing to bring them to ruin, but him who raises the fallen to lead them into glory.

We should rejoice exceedingly in this transformation, which brings us from earthly obscurity into heavenly dignity through the effects of the ineffable mercy of God, who descended all the way down to us in order to raise us all the way up to him.

SOLEMNITY OF THE ASCENSION*

Leo the Great, *Sermon 73, 2-4*

We are made for heaven and cannot fly low our entire lives. The weight of sin holds us anchored to the ground, bound to ourselves and to material things, but God's love draws us toward him delicately and sweetly. He does not break down the door to our hearts, because he has the key; but he wants us to rediscover the delight of opening ourselves from within and joyfully welcoming him.

The Ascension of Christ is thus our own elevation, and the hope of the body is likewise called to where the glory of the head has preceded us. Let us therefore allow our joy to erupt as it should, and let us rejoice in such a fervent movement of grace: indeed, today we were not only confirmed in the attainment of paradise, but we also penetrated through to the highest heights of heaven with Christ; we received more from the ineffable grace of Christ than what we had lost through the jealousy of the Evil One. Indeed, the Son of God incorporated into himself those whom the virulent Enemy had crushed after a first period of happiness, in order to give them a place later at the right hand of the Father.

---

* Regarding the Ascension of the Lord, the ecclesiastical provinces of Boston, Hartford, New York, Newark, Philadelphia, and Omaha have retained its celebration on the proper Thursday, while all other provinces have transferred this solemnity to the Seventh Sunday of Easter.

Thursday

Augustine, *On Faith, Hope, and Love*, 14, 53

We are the most well-to-do heirs: we are the favorite children of the merciful Father, witnesses to the Gospel who, through the virtues and sufferings of Christ, walk in the world carrying our crosses. Renewed in Baptism and abandoning sin, we live as risen men and women passing through this world with our feet on the ground, our hands outstretched toward our neighbors, and our gaze set on heaven.

A ll that happened on the Cross of Christ, in the tomb, during the Resurrection on the third day, during the Ascension into heaven, and at the throne at the right hand of the Father—all stands to represent Christian life, not just in words but also in actions. Indeed, it has been said regarding the Cross that "those who belong to Christ [Jesus] have crucified their flesh with its passions and desires" (Gal 5:24). Through his burial: we were buried together with Christ in Baptism, by which we die to the world. Through his Resurrection: just as Christ rose from the dead by the glory of the Father, we too walk in the newness of life. Through his Ascension into heaven and the throne at the right hand of the Father: if you have risen with Christ, seek the things of heaven, where Christ is seated at the right hand of the Father, and taste the things of heaven rather than those of the earth; indeed, you have died and your life is hidden with Christ in God.

FRIDAY

Gregory the Great, *Homilies*, 2, 29, 11

Jesus did not leave by ascending into heaven; in fact, he still makes himself present today as he did then. He has shown us the way, the truth, and the life, and he has left the Church to be a guide and teacher. We meditate, pray, and act within the Church to prevent the Gospel from remaining just a book like any other—collecting dust on the shelves or sitting on the ambo—and to allow it to walk the streets of the world with our legs.

Therefore, most dearly beloved brothers, we need to turn our hearts toward where we believe he ascended with his body. Let us avoid earthly desires, and may nothing down here give us pleasure any longer, for we have a Father in heaven. And we should ponder this very carefully, for he who ascended meekly into heaven will return terrifyingly, and all that he taught us with docility he will demand from us with severity. Therefore, let no one dismiss the necessary time for penance; may no one neglect to take care of himself while at the height of his strength, for our Redeemer will be as severe when he comes to judge us as he was patient with us before the judgment. Therefore, brothers, do this among yourselves and meditate diligently upon this. Even though your soul may still be uncertain, being shaken and confused by earthly passions, toss the anchor of your hope toward the eternal homeland now, fortify the resolutions of your soul in the true light. Here we have heard that the Lord ascended into heaven. Therefore, let us always meditate on what we believe in.

SATURDAY

Augustine, *Sermon 263, 2*

Thinking of heavenly things is the most sublime meditation for someone who has faith. It would be wonderful if at the end of our lives, ready and eager like young St. Dominic Savio before he took his last breath, we were able to say, "What a beautiful thing I see!" But God's wonders are already here on earth, among us and with us, so let us meditate upon what we expect to find in heaven while we are still on earth.

As you have heard, brothers, today our Lord Jesus Christ ascended into heaven: may our hearts also ascend with him. Let us listen to the Apostle, who says, "If then you were raised with Christ, seek what is above, where Christ is seated at the right hand of God. Think of what is above, not of what is on earth" (Col 3:1-2). Indeed, just as he ascended (into heaven) and did not leave us, so we too are already above with him, even though what was promised for our bodies has not yet occurred. He has already been raised high above the heavens. In truth, we should not give up on reaching the perfect and angelic heavenly resting place because of what he said: "No one has gone up to heaven except the one who has come down from heaven, the Son of Man" (Jn 3:13). But this was said because we are all united to him: indeed, he is our head, and we are his body. If, then, he ascends into heaven, we do not separate from him. He who descended from heaven does not deny us heaven, but in a certain sense he is saying, "Be my limbs if you wish to ascend into heaven." In the meantime, therefore, let us grow stronger in what we desire most profoundly.

Seventh Week of Easter and Pentecost

Sunday

John Cassian, *Conferences*, 21, 14-15

We can live the liturgical year, and this period in particular, as a sort of gym for the soul (and also for the body), training ourselves for a richer and more authentic experience of living in accordance with the Gospel. Where do we start? What equipment do we use? The program is already laid out, and the Sunday readings are certainly the starting point, but we also need to think with intelligence, to act with sound judgment, and to trust in the Holy Spirit.

K eeping vigils, reading the Sacred Scriptures, meditating, and above all fasting: we are divinely commanded by the authority of the Sacred Scriptures to dedicate ourselves to all of these activities; however, we are not held to such continuity that it would never be acceptable to interrupt them for a short time, or always necessary to observe them. Indeed, that which is imposed by precept brings about death for those who disobey; instead, that which is advised rather than commanded is beneficial if observed, but does not bring punishment if not observed. Thus, the observance of all of these things—or certainly some of them—was commanded by our elders with wisdom and sound judgment in accordance with the cause, place, manner, and time. Indeed, if they are carried out at a certain time and in a certain place, they are clearly good and fitting observances; if they are carried out in an inappropriate manner, they are futile and even harmful. For example, if someone decided to dedicate himself to austere fasting upon the arrival of a fellow brother, in whom Christ himself should be refreshed with love and embraced with a warm welcome, would he not be proving himself inhuman instead of acquiring religious merit?

MONDAY

John Chrysostom, *Homily on Holy Pentecost*, 1

Come, Holy Spirit, send us a ray of your light from heaven. Come, Father of the poor, come, giver of gifts and light of our hearts. Perfect consoler, gentle guest of the soul, most tender relief, rest in the midst of labor, shelter in the midst of heat, comfort in the midst of tears, O most blessed light, flood the hearts of your faithful. Without your strength, there is nothing in humanity without guilt. Wash what is dirty, water what is dry, heal what is bleeding. Bend what is rigid, heat what is cold, straighten what is crooked. Grant your holy gifts to your faithful who confide in you alone. Grant virtue and recompense, grant a holy death, grant eternal joy. (See Pentecost Sequence.)

In virtue of the Holy Spirit, we obtain pardon for our sins; through his action, we are purified of all impurities; through meditation on him—with the grace that comes from him—we turn from humans into angels. Nevertheless, we do not change our human nature at all, but something even more extraordinary happens: while remaining in our same dimension as always, we nonetheless also participate in the angelic state. Such is the power of the Holy Spirit! Just as a flame baking clay transforms it into a hard and durable body, so does the fire of the Holy Spirit work; indeed, when it descends upon a good soul, that soul becomes more solid than iron even if it appeared softer than unbaked clay up until that moment, and it makes a soul that was covered in the filth of sins a moment earlier more radiant than the sun.

Tuesday

Pseudo-Macarius, *Spiritual Homilies*, 18, 1-3

Praying to the Holy Spirit means recognizing the great treasure left by Christ for the Church and for all of us. Intense and constant prayer is the path to successfully respecting, with simplicity and firmness, all of the divine precepts that up until now were impossible for us to observe without the proper aid. No one can feel alone in his divine presence!

Therefore, anyone who has found and possesses this heavenly treasure of the Spirit carries out all things—thanks to him—according to the justice and virtue inspired by the commandments, far from all fault and preserved from any reproach, easily and effortlessly. We too therefore implore and beseech the Lord, that he might bestow on us the treasure of his Spirit: indeed, only in this manner will we be able, together with the aid of that heavenly abundance which is Christ himself, to act in accordance with all of God's commandments without stain or reproof, fulfilling with purity and perfection every demand for justice issuing forth from the Spirit. . . . Thus, it is essential that each of us unceasingly ask the Lord to be judged worthy of attaining and finding the heavenly gift of the Spirit.

WEDNESDAY

Basil the Great, *Homily on Faith*, 3

The Holy Spirit is the light that fills the Church and every Christian. Lavished with his seven gifts, we are called to be credible and courageous witnesses of the Gospel, bearers of light where there are shadows of sin, mistrust, misery, pain, and death. May the Spirit be the light of our consciences in our ordinary activities, in our daily choices, in the large and small concerns of life, and in moral and spiritual growth.

The Spirit fills the angels and archangels, sanctifies the powers, and gives life to all. He gives himself to all of creation; but he gives himself in different ways to different creatures, and he is not lessened by this participation in them. He gives his grace to all, but does not exhaust all that he is in any of those whom he graces; he fills to the brim those who receive him without losing anything. Just as the sun illuminates objects and gives itself to them in different ways without being diminished, so it is with the Spirit, who grants his grace to all while remaining intact and undivided. He enlightens all in their knowledge of God, excites the prophets, gives wisdom to lawmakers, consecrates priests, strengthens kings, perfects the just, makes the temperate worthy of honor, bestows the gift of holiness, raises the dead, frees captives, and makes foreigners his children.

Thursday

Augustine, *On Faith, Hope, and Love*, 14, 53

We are the most well-to-do heirs: we are the favorite children of the merciful Father, witnesses to the Gospel who, through the virtues and sufferings of Christ, walk in the world carrying our crosses. Renewed in Baptism and abandoning sin, we live as risen men and women passing through this world with our feet on the ground, our hands outstretched toward our neighbors, and our gaze set on heaven.

All that happened on the Cross of Christ, in the tomb, during the Resurrection on the third day, during the Ascension into heaven, and at the throne at the right hand of the Father—all stands to represent Christian life, not just in words but also in actions. Indeed, it has been said regarding the Cross that "those who belong to Christ [Jesus] have crucified their flesh with its passions and desires" (Gal 5:24). Through his burial: we were buried together with Christ in Baptism, by which we die to the world. Through his Resurrection: just as Christ rose from the dead by the glory of the Father, we too walk in the newness of life. Through his Ascension into heaven and the throne at the right hand of the Father: if you have risen with Christ, seek the things of heaven, where Christ is seated at the right hand of the Father, and taste the things of heaven rather than those of the earth; indeed, you have died and your life is hidden with Christ in God.

FRIDAY

Cyril of Jerusalem, *Catechetical Lectures XVI, 22-23*

Looking directly into the Sun with the naked eye is impossible, just as it is difficult to understand the way the Holy Spirit works in us without the lens of faith and without knowledge of the Gospel. Belief is the Christian's "yes" to God's proposal of a holy life, which comes to us through the intervention of the Paraclete, the defender, the advocate, the mediator, the love of the Father and the Son.

The Holy Spirit is someone magnificent, omnipotent, and extraordinary in the gifts he brings. . . . The Spirit acts efficaciously to the extent and in the manner which is most fitting to each person: being at the center, he knows each of our natures, discerning our thoughts and our conscience, everything we utter or that stirs up in our minds. . . . Like the light, which illuminates all things by emanating a single ray, so also the Holy Spirit illuminates those who have eyes to see him: indeed, if someone is considered unworthy of his grace and is therefore unable to perceive him, he should attribute the blame not to the Holy Spirit, but to his own lack of belief. Thus you have observed how the power of the Spirit extends throughout the universe; however, do not remain on the earth, but rise toward the heavens: ascend by your thoughts to the first heaven and contemplate the infinite myriads of angels residing there. . . . Well, God has placed the Paraclete at the head of all these as teacher and sanctifier.

SATURDAY

Cyril of Jerusalem, *Catechetical Lectures XVI*, 19-21

"Amen, amen, I say to you, no one can enter the kingdom of God without being born of water and Spirit. What is born of flesh is flesh and what is born of spirit is spirit. Do not be amazed that I told you, 'You must be born from above.' The wind blows where it wills, and you can hear the sound it makes, but you do not know where it comes from or where it goes; so it is with everyone who is born of the Spirit" (Jn 3:5-8). This is what John the Evangelist tells us from Nicodemus's encounter with Jesus. What was our encounter with Jesus like? Did we allow the light of the Spirit to light up the darkness of our hearts?

The work of the Holy Spirit aims exclusively at the fulfillment of justice and of salvation. His appearance is discreet at first, his grasp gentle, and his yoke soft. Emanations of light and knowledge announce his arrival beforehand. He arrives with the character of a true protector: indeed, he comes to bring salvation, to heal, to teach, to strengthen, to comfort, and to enlighten minds, first and foremost for the benefit of those who accept him, and then, through the work of the latter, for the benefit of others as well. And in the same manner as one whose eyes were first shrouded in darkness but then became illumined by the sudden appearance of the sun, allowing him to distinguish perfectly what he could not see prior to that moment, so he who has been considered worthy of receiving the Holy Spirit becomes enlightened in the depths of his soul and, in being raised above the human dimension, perceives what he had not known before then. While his body is still on earth, his soul is mirrored in the heavens.

PENTECOST SUNDAY

Irenaeus of Lyons, *Against Heresies*, 5, 9, 2-4

"'It will come to pass in the last days,' God says, / 'that I will pour out a portion of my spirit / upon all flesh. / Your sons and your daughters shall prophesy, / your young men shall see visions, / your old men shall dream dreams. / Indeed, upon my servants and my handmaids / I will pour out a portion of my spirit in those days, / and they shall prophesy. / And I will work wonders in the heavens above / and signs on the earth below: / blood, fire, and a cloud of smoke. / The sun shall be turned to darkness, / and the moon to blood, / before the coming of the great and splendid day of the Lord, / and it shall be that everyone shall be saved who calls on the name of the Lord'" (Acts 2:17-21).

Those who fear the Lord, who believe in the coming of his Son, and who keep the divine Spirit in their hearts with faith are truly men; they are clean and spiritual, and they live for God, because they possess the Spirit of the Father who purifies man and raises him to divine life. The Lord attests that the flesh is weak and the Spirit is ready (see Mt 26:41), meaning that it can do everything that is within its power. If what is within the power of the Spirit is united to the weakness of the flesh, the stronger necessarily overcomes the weaker, and thus the weakness of the flesh is absorbed by the strength of the Spirit. He who finds himself in this state is not physical but spiritual, because he is united to the Spirit. Therefore when the martyrs give their witness and disdain death, they are not acting according to their flesh, but in the strength of the Spirit.

. . . Hence, the flesh without the Spirit of God is dead, has no life, and cannot possess the Kingdom of God.

Irenaeus of Lyons, *Against Heresies*, 3, 17, 2-3

For fifty days, we have basked in the blessed euphoria of the Resurrection, celebrating the selfless gift of love and redemption. But the glory of the Easter event gradually begins to fade into memory like the forgotten coins that jingle in a pocket or purse, without purpose, without use. Pentecost reminds us that we need the Spirit, our Advocate, to feed the Easter fire within to give us strength and courage to put the coin of faith to work.

T*he Spirit of wisdom and understanding, the Spirit of counsel and strength, the Spirit of knowledge and the fear of God* came down upon the Lord, and the Lord in turn gave this Spirit to his Church, sending the Advocate from heaven into all the world into which, according to his own words, the devil too had been cast down like lightning.

If we are not to be scorched and made unfruitful, we need the dew of God. Since we have our accuser, we need an Advocate as well. And so the Lord in his pity for man, who had fallen into the hands of brigands, having himself bound up his wounds and left for his care two coins bearing the royal image, entrusted him to the Holy Spirit. Now, through the Spirit, the image and inscription of the Father and the Son have been given to us, and it is our duty to use the coin committed to our charge and make it yield a rich profit for the Lord.

ACKNOWLEDGMENTS

Scripture texts used in this work are taken from the *New American Bible,* copyright © 1991, 1986, and 1970 by the Confraternity of Christian Doctrine, Washington, DC 20017 and are used by permission of the copyright owner. All rights reserved.

Excerpts from the English translation of *The Liturgy of the Hours* © 1974, International Committee on English in the Liturgy, Inc. All rights reserved.

Permission to use other passages cited in this book was graciously provided by the publishers, to whom we express our thanks. Excerpts were translated directly from the Italian edition of this book:

> Bosio, G., E. Dal Covolo, and M. Maritano. *Introduzione ai Padri della Chiesa: Secoli III e IV* [Introduction to the Church Fathers: Third and Fourth Centuries]. Turin, Italy: SEI, 1993.

> Bosio, G., E. Dal Covolo, and M. Maritano. *Introduzione ai Padri della Chiesa—Secoli IV e V* [Introduction to the Church Fathers: Fourth and Fifth Centuries]. Turin, Italy: SEI, 1995.

Cyril and John of Jerusalem. *Le catechesi ai misteri* [Catecheses on the Mysteries]. Edited by A. Quacquarelli. Rome, Italy: Città Nuova, 1990.

Dorotheus of Gaza. *Insegnamenti spirituali* [Directions on the Spiritual Life]. Edited by M. Paparozzi. Rome, Italy: Città Nuova, 1993.

Starowieyski, M., and J. Miazek (eds.). *I Padri vivi* [The Living Fathers]. Rome, Italy: Città Nuova, 1982.

La teologia dei padri: Volume 2 [The Theology of the Fathers: Volume 2]. Rome, Italy: Città Nuova, 1974.

La teologia dei padri: Volume 3 [The Theology of the Fathers: Volume 3]. Rome, Italy: Città Nuova, 1975.

La teologia dei padri: Volume 4 [The Theology of the Fathers: Volume 4]. Rome, Italy: Città Nuova, 1975.

About the Author

Marco Pappalardo is a Salesian Cooperator, a past member of the National Council for Youth Pastoral Care of the Italian Bishops' Conference, and a member of the diocesan office for social communications of the Archdiocese of Catania, in Italy. He is a freelance journalist and author of several books in Italian. He is a literature teacher at Don Bosco High School in Catania.

INDEX OF CHURCH FATHERS